S. J. L.

Consolation, or, a Winter's Gleaning in a Poem

S. J. L.

Consolation, or, a Winter's Gleaning in a Poem

ISBN/EAN: 9783337256586

Printed in Europe, USA, Canada, Australia, Japan

Cover: Foto ©Thomas Meinert / pixelio.de

More available books at **www.hansebooks.com**

Consolation;

OR,

A WINTER'S GLEANING.

IN A POEM.

By S. J. L.

BOSTON:

PUBLISHED BY B. B. RUSSELL, 55 CORNHILL.

1871.

Rand, Avery, & Frye, Printers, Boston.

DEDICATION.

———◆———

TO some few of my friends to memory dear
   This work I offer, be they far or near ;
And if, in tracing these pages o'er,
They're reminded of days no more,
Of the pleasant hours we five have shared,
Then I am repaid for each line prepared.
Trusting to the loving-kindness of all,
I on your charity truly must call
To pardon the errors that uppermost lie :
They'll grieve, I know, the critical eye.
But not for the critic, be he good or wise,
Have I my heart-fancies bidden to rise,
But for those who lightened my lonely heart
When from home and loved ones doomed to part ;
Who by their tenderness sought to while
The tedious hours with song and with smile,
Nor sought in vain.   Hot tears fall fast
As I think of the four, loved till the last ;
And though mile upon mile our persons divide,
Our souls, united, walk closely beside.
Dear friends of my heart, though we ne'er meet more
Until we've crossed to the shining shore,
May the past, with its memories kind and sweet,
With its halo of love, rest at your feet,
Where I, with humble reverence, lay
The book that " HULDA " has written to-day !

APRIL 13, 1871.

CONTENTS.

6 CONTENTS.

CONSOLATION.

CHAPTER I.

THE WEDDING.

ALL the long day the pure and fleecy snow
   Had been softly falling down in flurries
White; while old Mount Grace was covered o'er
From base to crown with her spotless robe.
  All the little brooks that in summer-time
Babbled to the passer-by so gayly
And so free were hushed then and still;
For 'twas mid-winter, and in her chill embrace
All Nature rocked herself to sleep.

Some two miles out from the village street
Of dear old Warwick, — for there my stories lies
In its beginning, — there stood, and yet doth stand,
The pleasant farm-house of John Stevens,
A well-to-do farmer, kind and jolly,
Who loved to crack his joke with a neighbor,
And who loved his wife and his children well;
But some there were who said, perhaps with truth,

His idol and his pet was not his wife,
Nor either of his children ten, but his
Gray mare.
    Within the house, the busy housewife,
On many cares intent, sped back and forth
With a smiling face, but with weary feet;
For, when the evening came, Vira, her eldest,
The daughter of her youth, would leave her home
To share with him she'd chosen their future,
Be it weal or woe. Aunt Eunice and Thankful,
John's maiden sisters, were making wreaths
With which to deck the large old-fashioned room,
By courtesy called parlor; though we of modern times
Would smile to have so plain and barren room
Thus denominated.
The dark yet polished floor was carpetless,
Save here and there a home-made rug.
    The ample fireplace, from whence pleasant warmth
Permeated all the room, reflected back
The brightening glow of the great fire-dogs,
Polished so highly, they seemed like mirrors.
    In the far-off corner stood the guest-bed,
With its silken curtains flowing loosely
From the wainscoted ceiling to the floor;
A wooden settee, covered with gorgeous patch,
Graced another corner; while close beside
Stood the three-legged light-stand, with the Bible,
A century old, lying on it year by year.
    A large old-fashioned bureau with brass handles
Also pressed against the wall: above it
Hung the "family record," wrought by Vira
When only eleven: its companion-piece
Represented a milkmaid and green cows,

Blue grass, and yellow skies, purple roses,
And all the *et cæteras* that form a *gay* picture.
   The one rocking-chair, and seat of honor,
Stood in the middle of the floor :
In the corner next the fire stood the clock,
Tall and shining in its oaken dress ;
And its long brass pendulum kept swinging
The same old tune, — " Never, forever,
   Never more ! "
With the evening came the wedding-guests,
Who, despite the falling snow and threatened drifts,
Were in their gayest humor : while above,
In the girls'-room, a merry group displayed .
Their love and pretty taste as they arrayed
The bride in her soft gray silk, trimmed with lace ;
While she, trembling with mingled joy and fear,
Repaid their teasing raillery of wit
With pleased yet silent smiles.
   Upon the stair falls now a manly tread ;
And " May I come ? " is knocked upon the door.
" Oh, yes ! " the laughing damsels cry ; and then
Upon the threshold of the door stands James,
The bridegroom, so young, so fair and manly,
Who, turning to his bride-elect, with arms
Outstretched, holds her in a close embrace.
Pressing with his lips her lofty brow,
He murmured low, " May God ne'er smile on me
If I henceforth keep not the vows which I
To-night do take upon myself ! " — " We're waiting ! "
Called forth the youngest brother from below :
So the bridal party passed down the stairs,
And quietly arranged themselves in the centre
Of the room, before the chair of state, in which

Good Parson Jones had been resting an hour
Or more, cracking a joke or two with zest
Among the merry guests assembled there.
    A few brief words, an earnest prayer, and then
Vira Stevens was no more.   A husband
Now claimed full allegiance from her heart;
And, though the tears filled her eyes when she saw
Her mother's orbs o'erflowing with tender love,
She quickly drove them back, and gazed in pride
Upon her love and master, James Horton,
To her seeming the very prince of men ;
" And all went merry as a marriage-bell."
    The storm-clouds, which all day
Had disgorged their fleecy contents, now broke,
Drifting from each other far and wide apart,
Letting in 'twixt their rifts the bright-eyed stars ;
While, slowly climbing overhead, the moon,
Night's fair and radiant queen, the heavens
Seemed to light into a brilliance most fair.
At last, when ten o'clock had slowly chimed
The hour, the guests, including bride and groom,
Were making their adieus ; while Aunt Eunice
With hearty good will threw after the bridal pair
An old slipper, — " for good luck," she said.
    The happy twain, thus escorted by friends,
Soon reached their own snug home ; and therein peace
And the bliss of wedded life we leave them.

CHAPTER II.

SARAH'S CHILDHOOD.

FIVE years of mingled joy and pain have passed
  Since Vira left the dear parental roof
Of her childhood's home. Now a little babe
Has come to bless her with its infant smiles ;
A little daughter, which she has christened
Sarah, — to her name ever dear, since 'twas
Her mother's. The father his disappointment
Could scarce conceal because his daughter dear
Was not a son ; for on that ideal
He had rested his fondest hopes for years.
  Alas ! poor Vira had much need of comfort,
Since she was wedded scarce a year e'er she
Discovered she had indeed a rival,
And one much to be feared ; since passion hot
And fierce assailed her with this demon wild,
Who often seemed to tear at the very strings
Of her heart. Oh the agony of soul
She felt when first she knew that James,
Her idol and her liege lord, was subject
To the demon drink ! Prayers and tears alike
Seemed powerless to stem his downward walk
Into that abyss of shame, — a drunkard's grave.

And so the weary years rolled on,
Till fifteen summer-suns had cast their brightness
Over Sarah's face ; when, one wild autumnal night,

James Horton, the husband and father,
Was from a drunken frolic brought home dead.
   The shock to poor Vira's nerves was fearful,
Quite unnerving her for all life's sterner tasks :
Thus a double burden fell on Sarah,
Who bravely struggled with her adverse fate,
And by her kind solicitude and care
Smoothed from her mother's path each bitter thorn.
   But Vira's life hung by a brittle thread ;
And, after many a long and serious talk
With the family physician, she one night
Called her daughter to her side, praying
That she might bear the burden given her
For some wise purpose from the Father's hand.
   Resting her white and slender hand with love
Upon her daughter's brow, she thus began :
" For fifteen years, my Sarah, you have been
To me the one bright centre of my heart ;
The one for whom I've wrought and toiled
With purpose strong and high : many a time
Have you stood betwixt me and harm, when he,
Your father, knew not what mad acts he wrought.
   " On one sad night, when he with fury wild
Approached me with a hatchet keen,
I held you up before his face, and cried,
' O James ! see your little daughter's face :
You will not, surely, harm your child ? '
' No,' said he ; ' the child is safe : but I wish
In darkest Hades was its mother.'
My Sarah, can you guess the bitter grief
That filled your mother's heart in those sad days ?
And yet it was not always so.   At first,
Your father was as kind and good a man

As you would often see : but for a friend
He bound himself for all that he was worth,
And more ; and, through falsehood vile, this friend
Defrauded him of all he had.
And then his courage, and his faith in man,
Vanished like the mists of morning : and so,
To banish his discomfiture, he took to drink ;
And, seething his brain with the vile poison,
He was not accountable for his deeds.

"He was my husband, the father of my child :
And so, despite the urgent wish of all
My friends, I staid with him until the last ;
Often going supperless to bed,
And sometimes shivering with cold. And you
Would put your precious arms about my neck,
Pressing with your own my tear-wet cheek,
And whisper, ' Don't cry, mamma ! don't you cry !'
Thus have you been my solace and my hope.

" For many years I've shared your daily presence ;
But now it seemeth best that we should part.
Your education is indifferent ; and I wish
To place you for two years in Madam R.'s
Graduating-school for young ladies ;
Because, my child," — and now did Vira's voice
Grow low and tender, — " I deem that it is best
You should know that Dr. Walton and others
Think you may at any hour become
An orphan child indeed. My heart, they say,
Is much diseased ; and I must be .prepared
To bid farewell to life most suddenly.'

" Could I but feel assured that you were well,
And happily provided for, I'd be
Content to submit to the Father's will ;
But love for you ofttimes makes me rebel.   •

2

" If the wealth that once was ours
Could dower you with a competency,
'Twould be so much for you ; but now, alone
And poor, a harder path your feet must tread.
'Tis now Thanksgiving week ; and, when shall come
The Christmas holidays, we two must learn
To live apart."
    " O mamma ! if what you tell me is true,
I cannot leave you here and alone :
No comfort could I take, though much I'd like
To garner knowledge, for 'tis the key of power.
No, mamma : let me stay with you to cheer
Your last remaining days with deeds of love."
    " Not so, dear child," Vira quick replied.
" I shall not be alone ; for your grandpa
Stevens is urging me to come and dwell
Once more beneath the dear, parental roof.
Besides, necessity almost compels me to :
Since all we have will barely pay your board
And tuition for the terms I've set for you ;
And, as this is all I can to you bequeath,
An education you must have.
    " Yesterday I spoke to Melinda Jones,
Good old Parson Jones's youngest daughter,
To come and cut and make for you
Whate'er is needful for your coming use :
We have so much to do, we cannot waste
Our time in tears.   And now, my darling girl,
Kiss me good-night ; and remember, dear,
You ever have your mother's love and blessing."

CHAPTER III.

THE VOW.

A MID the mountains of the Verd-mont State,
    Nestling like the tiny violet from sight,
Lies the pretty town of W.
In the large two-story house, a little back
From the main street, a young wife and mother
Is battling for her life.
Slowly she turns her death-filmed eyes
Upon each tearful face; then beckoning
To one sister dearer than the rest, whose hand
She clasped with dying strength, she wildly cried,
" Glencora, do you love me ?   Then listen ;
And, if you'd have me die in peace, you'll grant
This my last request. — Charles, come hither too :
Now take Glencora's hand in yours, and promise
Both of you, when I've been dead a year,
That you will marry : so this darling boy
May have a mother, who will love him
For his dead mother's sake."
    The two, thus strangely and solemnly addressed,
Gazed with awe into each other's face ;
Neither feeling much inclined to speak.
" Speak, I do implore ! " the dying woman cried :
" My moments fast are ebbing out, and you
Will not ease their pain !   Glencora, oh, say
That you will be a mother to my child ! "
    Then did this sister, nobly renouncing

Self and selfish feelings, make the vow
That henceforth shattered her own bright hopes;
For well she knew another held the place
A husband alone should ever claim.

   Solon Gordon was a clergyman of the
Episcopalian order, and in the town
Of W. had lived some two years or more.
Tall and commanding in stature, he walked
A very prince 'mong men. His broad, full brow
Showed the intellect hidden there;
His eyes, so soft and dark, seemed wells of thought;
About his mouth there was a pleasant smile;
And his deep-toned voice rang out like music.
All the people loved him far and near,
He was so gentle and so good; and he it was
Glencora had resigned to soothe the dying
Wish of one who now could see how great
Her sacrifice had been.
While yet that sister lay shrouded below,
Glencora, with an aching heart, a letter
Wrote to him, blotted o'er with tears;
And thus the missive ran: —

   " My dearest now, as you evermore will be,
I know not how or where to begin this
My last and farewell letter unto you:
For though our wedding-day is set, and we
So many blissful plans have for the future
Made, it now must all be blotted out
As though it ne'er had been; for I to-night
Have made a vow, to calm a dying soul,
That raises a barrier high 'twixt you and me.
  ." I hope some worthier one and happier
Far than I can ever be will make to you

Amends for all I've done amiss:
And, though I may not be your wife, your friend
Most firm and faithful I will ever be;
And God, dear friend, well knows 'tis not because
I love you less I give you now this pain.
And much I hope your prayers 'll help us both
To bear the heavy cross I almost loathe.
    " Do not forsake me, dearest; and remember
You are, as you have ever been, the best
And dearest of God's creatures in my eyes.
And, oh! thank him, with me, *this life* is not
For always.   There dawns another day,
When all the parted here shall meet ' up there '
To glorify our Lord. — GLENCORA."

    The morning sun of a chill November day
Threw its brightening gleams across the brow
Of the young minister as he in his
Quiet study sat.
Within his slender hand the golden pen
Still held the drop of ink just dipped
Into its hollow palm, when a gentle rap
Upon the door proclaimed a visitor;
And to his kind response of " Come," Betty,
His old friend and faithful nurse,
With a smiling face, handed him the letter
From Glencora; at sight of which his face
Lighted up to a beauty rare.   And then
He took the missive dear, and kissed it o'er
And o'er, because, forsooth, her dear hand
Had lately pressed it.   Carefully he cut
One end of it apart, loitering like a child
O'er the sweetmeats it has coveted,

2*

While his lips softly murmured, "My darling!
God keep me from loving thee too well."
   His eyes had travelled half way down the sheet,
When a cold tremor seemed to shake his frame.
Twice he read the cruel missive over, —
Cruel, because it blighted in their freshest
Bloom two fond hearts. Dry and tearless sobs
Swelled his heart almost to suffocation ;
While on his brow, from which the waves of hair
Were pushed so carelessly, the drops of keen
And bitter anguish stood.
   "O God ! why hast thou forsaken me ?" he cried.
" And must I thus resign my one ewe-lamb, —
The only one I have, save thee, in all
This earth ?   Can I see another claim   .
From her a wife's fond duty ? know her kiss,
Which I yet can feel upon *my* brow,
Henceforth rests upon another's face ?
Can I meet her eyes, sweet mirrors of the soul,
And crush out from my own the fond desire
My soul must ever feel to call her mine ?
Can I ever clasp her hand, and not feel
The sweet electric sympathy that thrills
Between us two ?   To meet in the common
Walks of life only as friends !   O Jesus !
Who by thy bloody sweat and agony
Didst bear the cross for such as me, listen
To my cry, and make this trial, so
Bitter now, to prove some day for my good.
And she, my poor Glencora ! — oh ! give her
Strength to bear the burden she takes upon
Herself, thinking, poor child ! she is doing
Her duty now ; although, most unhappily,

She is making, not only for herself,
But others, a weary bed of thorns,
Unsolaced by the priestess of a true
Home, — the goddess of love.
" As all is over between us two,
'Tis best we should not meet again ; and so
I'll ask leave of absence for a time,
Getting my old chum, Albert Nevers,
To take charge of my flock for me.   I am not fit
For any duty now ; but, in other
And far different scenes, my mind
May be eventually restored to its olden
Calm at least : but happiness seems ever
Removed from my path."

At luncheon-time, he astonished the faithful
Betty by saying he wished her to pack some
Linen changes in his valise : for he
On the morning train was going away.
His hasty preparations were soon made ;
His letter to his friend written, and
To which an answer of acceptance came.
Then he from an inner pocket of his coat
Drew forth a lady's face framed in golden case,
Upon which he gazed long and earnestly :
And to the thought arising in his heart
He quick replied, " No, no ! I cannot yet
Return this treasure dear, my bonnie bride,
My sweet, blue-eyed Glencora."   The present hour
With its bitterness o'erwhelmed his soul ;
And the strong man leaned his head upon
The table-slab, weeping bitterly.

CHAPTER IV.

THE HOSPITAL.

THE city of Newbern, North Carolina,
    Held in possession by the victorious
Army of the North, on the fifteenth of March
Presented a sad spectacle of dead
And wounded soldiers.
Hospitals were gotten up
In *impromptu* style for the suffering men ;
And, though all was done by the humane
Surgeons that circumstances would allow,
The suffering of those heroes brave was
Intense.   Many a fond Northern woman's
Heart has shed tears of bitter grief for those
Dear lads who went from almost every home ;
Many to suffer the tortures of captivity
And death.   No pen or imagination,
Be it e'er so prolific, can picture
The daily struggles of those to whom toil
And hardship were once things unknown.
In the present contest for the city
Of Newbern, four hundred and sixty-six
Gallant men were wounded, and ninety-one
Had passed on to that unseen land from whence
No traveller returns to tell us
Of the quiet meadows watered by the
River of Life ; of the beautiful mounts, whose peaks
Seem crusted o'er with gold and vermilion ;

Above the streets of shining jasper, so pure
In holiness, no sin can enter there.
    In the month of May, the slant rays of the
Afternoon sun fell across the row
Of single cots in the hospital-ward
Of number eight.   The thin pale faces
Of those lying there lighted up as they
Heard the echo of the doctor's step going
His evening rounds.   Presently their door swung
Quietly upon its hinges, disclosing
To their view the hospital-surgeon,
Accompanied by a tall, noble-looking
Man, dressed in clerical black, whom they all
Denominated " a parson," and whom most
Of them rejoiced to see ; the attention
Of this stranger being kindly directed
By the humane physician to those who
Had suffered most by their heroic valor
In their country's cause.   Here, as elsewhere,
Some there were who could not admit the truth
Of divine justness in their present trials.
    When this young soldier of the cross turned from
One and another of those maimed and crippled
Men, he thought it was hard indeed to talk
To *them* of submission and patience, since
They were living monuments of a fealty
Most loyal ; and yet he felt he could not
Leave them there in their wounded state without
Conveying to their souls the promises
Of the Saviour, crucified for their sake.
    One man, who seemed older than the rest,
Since his closely-shaven hair had turned gray,
With wistful earnestness watched the visitor,

Until at last he stood before his
Narrow cot: and when the surgeon, turning
Down the sheet, disclosed the stumps of his poor
Handless arms, the tears rolled down the face
Of our old friend Solon Gordon; for he,
To forget his own keen trial, had sought,
By ministering to the deeper woes of
The suffering about him, to lighten
As far as possible the wearisome hours
Of the inmates of the various hospital-
Wards.   Taking from his pocket a Common
Prayer Book, he was proceeding to
Open it: when the soldier cried, " You needn't
Do that; I want to hear none of your cant!
If God is wise and just, as you pious
Ones pretend, why did he let this war
Sweep over the country, bringing ruin
And death to so many homes?
Does he give me back my two hands?
Restore from their early graves my sons, —
The three brave boys! — who, filled with valor
For their country's wrongs, so bravely fought,
And, fighting, died?   Will he restore to my
Dear old wife the husband and sons
Of her youth, and make the bread to ripen
Without labor at her feet?   I tell you,
No, no! instead, this fair and pleasant land
Will be strewn with the dead and dying.
The war is only just begun: there will
Be scarce one home in all the States, North or
South, but that shall be made to mourn.   And why?
Where is the justice of it?   I don't see
Why the good and poor must suffer for the

Sins of the rich and wicked ones.   And I
Say again, there *is no* God of justice
Or mercy, or he would not allow
Such things to be; and so, as I don't believe,
You needn't waste your prayers on me.
There is one in the corner there, who is
Almost through with this world, and to whom you,
Perhaps, will be a welcome messenger."
  By advice of this blunt, outspoken old man,
Our friend slowly passed down the narrow space
Allotted between the two rows of cots
Until he gained the spot designated.
Lying before him was a young man,
Evidently some twenty-two years of age,
And upon whose manly face cruel Death
Had already set his seal.   In his eyes
There gleamed a peaceful light of contentment.
  He grasped the minister's hand as though
Welcoming a long-known friend; so quickly
Can the soul intuitively perceive
Those who are congenial.   The physician
Seemed to think it would be best, perhaps,
To leave the ward and its occupants
To their usual rest and quietude;
And in the morn, as early as he liked,
He could come again.   Bidding his new friend
A kindly farewell, he left him with the
Promise of coming on the morrow, God willing.

CHAPTER V.

THE DYING SOLDIER.

THE morning of the sixteenth of May found
Solon Gordon seated by the simple
Yet wholesome cot-bed of William King,
Whose sallow face lighted up with vivid
Pleasure when he saw his kind visitor
Of the previous day had not forgotten
To fulfil his promise; which, alas!
Too many are prone to do.
After the morning salutations had
Been exchanged between the two, Gordon took
The Prayer Book, which he opened, turning
With thoughtful hand to the one hundred
And thirtieth Psalm, commencing,
" Out of the deep have I called unto thee,
O Lord ! Lord, hear my voice."
By request of the sick man, he went through
With the usual morning service, bearing,
As it seemed, upon the wings of faith,
The weary soul of him who listened, to
The very throne of grace. At its close,
Stretching forth his hand, the sick man cried,
" Bless you for your kindness to one unknown,
And but a simple soldier too !
Forgive me if your kindness I shall over-
Tax ; but they tell me, sir, my lease of life
Has most run out. You seem to me a good

Man and a true; and so if you will be
So kind as to take charge of these for me," —
Drawing from beneath his pillow two small
Packets, — " and deliver them to the ones
Addressed, when I am in my Southern grave,
Then will you indeed make my last moments
Happy by your deed of charity.

  " This package, tied with a strip of green,
Belongs to my mother, who is a widow
In the bustling town of B.,
In the State of Vermont.   'Twill be a sad
Day for her when she learns her eldest boy,
The pride of her fond heart, has run his race
So quickly here; though thus she prophesied
'Twould be.   This one, banded with the blue,
Goes to Amy Norton, my old school-chum,
The dear competitor in all my classes,
And who by my side I had hoped, fondly,
Some day in the future to win for my
Own sweet wife.   These are her letters and
Dear pictured face; and here upon my
Heart rests the golden tress she gave me
The sad morn we parted.   And tell her,
Too, — for she will prize that more than the
Rest, — that her teaching and her prayers
At last prevailed; and I now believe
In the Father and the Son and the
Holy Ghost, — the three in one combined.
She knows how sceptical I used to be,
Often wounding her by my ill-timed jests
Of the rarity of Christian men;
Judging, as too many are prone to do,
The whole by the faithlessness of the few.

3

She, dear girl! has had bitter trials to
Contend against.   Her mother died when she
Was but an infant child; and her father,
Being left with many little ones
Upon his hands, soon married again, —
One who was, most unfortunately, unkind
To him and them: so she really had no
Home, no mother's kindly influence
To guide her in the path of rectitude.
Her aspirations were of a nature
Lofty, and not easily dispelled.
Outstripping all her mates in the common
School, she resolved to attend the large
And flourishing academy in the town
Adjoining : so various methods she
Contrived to earn the wherewithal
With which to pay her board and tuition.
  "I need not tell you how diligently
She toiled: oftentimes the midnight-hour
Found her still poring o'er her books.   Rivals
From the first were we : but soon a warmer
And more earnest feeling filled my heart
For her; and there was nothing, no sacrifice
I would not make for her dear sake ; and so
Our friendship ripened into love faithful
Unto death.   The hardest thought of all
To me is this, — I never more shall meet
The sunny glance of her large blue eyes,
Nor gaze upon that brow so broad and full ;
Ne'er listen more to her mellow voice so
Clear, nor feel the pressure of her hand
Upon my own tired brow.   But God is good,
And he will care for her as well as me ;

Will lead her feet o'er pastures fittest for
Her need.   Tell her I have done my duty here
To the best of the powers given me;
Shrinking not from toil, howe'er hard and
Distasteful it might be; and at the last
I die resigned to my fate, well knowing
For some good purpose 'tis wisely ordered."
    Sharp spasms of pain now contracted Will
King's face; and, after passing him the cordial,
Gordon said, " As you are so weary now,
I will leave you, and come again at night."
    Smiling assent, the dying soldier closed
His weary eyes, hoping to gain some rest.

At the evening hour, the minister was
Wending his way adown the length of ward
Number eight.   The moment his eye rested
Upon the face of William King, he knew
The hours of his life were numbered:
About his mouth and nose was the blue, pinched
Look which ever indicates the dread reality
Of death.   With a smile he greeted the new-
Found friend, hoarsely murmuring, " You've come
Just in time to see me die.   I am so glad
Not to be alone! though I am not that;
For the room seems full of angels.   Hark, hark!
Did you not hear that strain of music rare?
They're coming near and nearer: glory be
To thee, thou Lord of all! "   And, raising
His hands in an ecstasy of delight,
His eyes set; when with one spasmodic
Effort he gasped, " Dear mother! Amy!
Blessed! "— and, with the utterance of that

Last word, the spirit of William King passed
From its prison-house of clay up to the   ·
Paradise of the happy souls made free.

The next morn, at an early hour, the burial-
Service for the dead was read over the
Cold body of another gallant hero,
Who, in the morning of youth, gave his health
And life for the preservation of our
War-stained land.
Feeling that his mission recalled him
Elsewhere, Solon Gordon bade farewell to
Newbern, bearing with him the dead soldier's
Messages of love, and the packages
Which he was to deliver to the mother
And the dearest friend of the deceased.

CHAPTER VI.

THE MISSION.

THE thriving town of B., not far distant
From the Massachusetts line, was the home
Of William King's mother, who, by the death
Of this son, would be indeed bereft, — with
Only one child left, and he of not much
Promise.   Gordon felt his courage fail
Most rapidly when he found himself at
Last before the widow's door; for nought he
Dreaded more than a woman's tears.
When his sad, brief story had been told, she
Calmly thanked him for his kindness to her
Son; assuring him with broken voice,
That, though she could not reward him, there was
One who would.   Reminding her that she must
Henceforth believe she had a friend in him,
Upon whom she could depend in case of need.
He, with cordial hand-clasp, bowed himself away,
Questioning in his mind if every woman's
Heart was as firm as seemed the one
Of this middle-aged lady, so tearless,
Yet so stricken.
The first day of June, which was a bright and
Odorous one, the dead soldier's messenger
Found himself in the small and common-
Looking reception-room of a large and
Fashionable boarding-house.

3*

To the servant he gave his card; waiting
Meanwhile, with a strange desire, to see
The face of her who filled so completely
The young hero's ideal of a woman.
Presently he heard the soft rustle of
A dress upon the stair.　Turning his back
To the opening door, the visitor
Felt that mysterious fascination
Which some souls ever exert upon
Sympathetic powers.　He turned and bowed,
Saying, " Miss Norton, I presume," as she,
Advancing, met his outstretched hand.
" Will you be seated, please ; and tell me, pray,
Why I am thus indebted for your call."
　　Viewing her with a critic's eye, Gordon
Saw that she was fair and sweet and young ; and,
Better still, that truth and purity looked
Forth from those lovely eyes of blue : her brow
Was high and full ; her nose, the short Grecian ;
While about her mouth, the sweetest feature
Of the face, much tenderness, yet firmness,
Seemed to lie : then her chin was not pointed
Nor retreating, but rounded and dimpled ;
Her hair was in the shadow brown, golden
In the sun ; her figure round and flexible ;
And, taken as a whole, she was as sweet
A type of womanhood as one would care
To see.　" Dear lady," he answered, speaking
Very low, " I bring you news of a friend
Who held you most dear, and whose memory
Will ever treasured live within your heart.
I speak of William King, who on his dying-
Bed gave me this, and bade me bring it you,

And with it his best love ; also to tell
You that he'd done his duty well, dying
At last, trusting and believing in the God
Whom you adore ; and all through your dear faith.
  " I saw him die, and with these hands softly
Closed his eyelids down. I saw him laid in the
Soldier's grave, and marked the spot with a wooden
Cross, lettered ' W. K. ; twenty-two ; May
Sixteenth.' " All the time, Amy had sat like
Some marble image without soul ; but, when
Gordon arose to go, she made efforts
Strong to command herself. But, alas ! the
Strain upon her nerves was too great : fainting,
She fell at his feet. Very tenderly
He laid her upon the sofa, sprinkling
Water upon her face till she revived.
Then the re-action came : sobs wild and deep
Shook her frame in convulsive throes. The friend
At first nothing said ; but, after the
Violence of her grief had spent itself,
He again repeated the facts of her dear friend's
Happy death, comforting her with the sweet
Promises of the Lord, that all " those who
Die in Jesus shall meet again."
Taking her hand in parting, he asked her
" To rely upon him as a friend ; and
He wished that she would write sometimes to him,
And let him know how fate was using her : "
To all of which she promised.

And how, meantime, has fared Glencora,
The once promised bride of the wandering
Minister ? As the weeks slowly lapsed,

She felt more and more the wickedness
Of entering into vows she never
Could accept with truth.   Two letters she had
Written to Gordon, claiming his pardon
And return, — letters fraught with tenderest
Language from her heart, but which he never
Had received.   Now he had returned, seeming
To her eyes dearer than before.   Sometimes
She thought she would write him yet again ; but
Pride forbade : and so the weeks rolled on
Until the autumn came, rich with fruitage
And with flowers.   One fair autumnal eve,
At the closing of the week, the minister,
Returning from a pleasant but lonely
Stroll, was met at the door by his faithful
Betty, who announced that " a lady all
In black was waiting in the study for
His return."   Little thinking who was his
Guest, he quietly entered the room ; and
At first it seemed vacant, as the gloom
Of the twilight hour concealed from view
The form of the trembling woman,
Who, advancing, threw herself at his feet,
Crying, " Have you indeed forgotten your
Glencora, who, humbly kneeling at your feet,
Implores forgiveness for the past, and love
For the future ?   I cannot live without
You, my darling and my pride : nothing
In this life seems worth the having, bereft
Of you.   I'd rather live in the poorest
Hovel, upon some lone mountain, as *your wife*,
Than be the titled mistress of thousands,
With countless servants to heed my slightest

Call.   When I promised you to forsake,
I thought it was my duty: but, alas!
I've found 'twould be a trespass upon the
Holiest laws of God and man should I
Persist in keeping that mad vow; for I
Love him not, save as the father of my
Sister's child ; and she in paradise doth
Surely know how utterly wrong the keeping
Of her wish would be.   My pride I've humbled ;
And here I am suing for your dear love,
The best and richest gift earth can on me
Bestow.   Gordon, dear one, oh! say you'll not refuse
Your poor Glencora ! "
" Refuse you? no', my darling!" quoth he :
" You are much too sweet and dear a treasure
To my heart for a resistance to your
Love. 'For months I've sought to blot your image
From my soul ; but never has there dawned
A day or hour that I have not thought of
You, my treasure sweet."   And, bending low,
He raised her from his feet, resting her head
Upon his breast, her face bathing with the
Happy drops of joy, and then softly kissing
Them away.   The blissful silence that e'er
Falls between the long parted and re-united
Ones fell upon them in that hour of peace.

CHAPTER VII.

OCTOBER the sixteenth was the time
    Re-appointed by Glencora for the
Consummation of their marriage.   The guests
Were invited, the wedding-garments made,
And the bride-cake was ready for the knife ;
When, like a two-edged sword to the young
Pastor, came another note from Glencora,
Saying she once again had proved traitor
To her vows, and all must drop at the
Eleventh hour : not one word the reason
To assign ; leaving him and others to
Their own conjectures.
This was, in truth, the hardest trial he
Had yet been called upon to bear.   He felt
'Twas neither wise nor best for him to longer
Tarry in the place where twice he had been
Duped by the loving words of a woman
Unstable as water, and whose conduct
Would cast a seeming disgrace upon his
Character.   He at once called a parish-
Meeting, simply asking them for a quick
Dismissal, which was without a murmur
Granted ; for the people were sensitive
To their minister's misfortune.

Once more was Gordon a wanderer,
Roaming from place to place where'er his feet,

So restless, were guided by the hand of Fate.
At last he thought of Amy Norton, from
Whom he had heard by letter, it is true;
But the sympathy of whose sweet face
He felt would now be doubly precious.
Speedily his way he wended to the
Inland town where she resided; and, when
He had clasped in his her welcoming hand,
He felt as though he had indeed a friend
In that dear woman. He came again, and
Yet again, the souls of each grown nearer
From their frequent intercourse of thought;
Until at last he shaped into words the
One thought that in his dormant heart
Had struggled into life : and thus it was
He showed her all his heart, telling her
With tearful eyes of high hopes blighted, and
The heart's fondest affections chilled, by the
Fickle nature of one woman's caprice.
He had loved her, oh, so much! yet she duped
And betrayed him. "Perhaps," he said, "he'd made
Of her too fond an idol, forgetting
The Creator in the creature; but now
'Twas all a dream of the past, sweet and pleasant,
But with the life before him shared no part.
She had suffered too, therefore could enter
Into all his feelings. Sympathy was sweet,
And there were many things between themselves
Congenial. The warmest friendship and
Respect stirred the hearts of both, each for each;
And why should they not unite their broken
Lives in the strong, endearing cord of
Matrimony? They thus could lighten each

The other's woe, and be the best of friends ;
Since reason would guide their actions, and not
The wild delirium of love."
To this mild philosophy fair Amy gave
Assent ; and they right speedily were
Married, and enjoying the peaceful rest
Of a Platonic love.　In course of time,
Four children — three sons and a daughter dear —
Brightened their home, and strengthened the placid
Friendship of the two so happily united.
　　Soon after leaving W., he had a call
To preside over a parish in the
City of Albany, New York ; and there
Until the death of his gentle Amy,
Which transpired when the tiny Sarah
Was a sedate little miss of two years,
He had lived, laboring for his Master's
Cause.　Fortune had not been lavish of her
Smiles.　Once the little parsonage and all
Its contents were burned to the ground ;
And, though his parishioners were most kind,
They could not to him restore his library,
Made dear from memories of the past.
In less than a year after his wife's decease,
His second son " passed over the river,
'Yond the tide ; " and soon, following him, his
Little daughter " sailed away with the boatman
Pale : " and so his household joys were wrested
From his clasping arms of love.
Feeling that home was now home no longer,
He sent his eldest son to live with his
Grandparents, keeping his youngest
(And the inheritor of his name) with him.

From city to city, to country town
And village, they roamed, — the father and son
Ever inseparable.   Years would be consumed
In following them in their various
Sojournings: so we will leave them to fate,
While we look after other characters
Of our story who have been too long
Neglected.

4

CHAPTER VIII.

SARAH HORTON.

YEARS have placed their record upon
The book of Time since Sarah entered Madam
R.'s "Seminary for Young Ladies," —
The first two years as a pupil,
Afterward as an assistant-teacher.
She had been there some twenty-two months, when
She one night received a despatch from her
Grandpa Stevens, saying, "Come home at once:
Your mother is dead!" Oh, dreadful words to
A loving child! — *your mother is dead!*
Volumes seem written in that one phrase.
Sarah immediately gave notice
To the principal of the school; and 'mid
The tears of her classmates and teachers, all
Of whom had learned to love her, she quickly
Departed on her sorrowful journey.
But not alone was she. The teacher of
Mathematics, a quiet and scholarly
Man, had thoughtfully followed her, and,
In his gentle way, soothed much of her grief;
Presenting to her view the beauty of
The life beyond, and that, instead of our
Feeling so unreconciled to the departure
Of those our hearts hold dear, we should esteem
It a blessing for them, if not for us.
Rapidly as the train moved, it yet seemed

To the sorrowing girl freighted with lead ; when
Suddenly the cars with a frightful leap
Went crashing through a bridge into the
Cold, blue waters of the Connecticut.
The sickening details of that sad, sad
Catastrophe, no pen can describe.
Four were killed, and seventeen wounded ; and
Among the dead was the kind friend who had
So tenderly befriended her in her
Sorrow, and who, they told her, had stood between
Her and death, as his head had been pressed
Against the stone butments of the bridge, where
Hers would naturally have fallen had he
Not thrown his arm about her, — giving for
Her life his own.   One of her arms was broken,
Her left ankle sprained, with some cuts upon
Her face.   The nearest houses were turned
Into hospitals.   Where Sarah was left,
Five gentlemen and three ladies were brought, —
Some in the most critical condition.
The present hour was to our heroine
The climax of her sorrows, since she now
Could not reach home in season to see once
Again her dear, dead mother's face ; for on
The morrow would be the funeral ; and she
Could not be moved for some days, and perhaps
Weeks, the attending surgeon said.
·   Meanwhile, sharing her own couch, was a young
Lady from Illinois, who had been on a
Visit to some friends in Springfield, Mass.
She was severely suffering from a
Spinal injury received in the late
Disaster.   Yet her fortitude and patience

Seemed to Sarah and to others as something
Almost divine.   Her lovely face, though pale
From suffering, seemed lighted with a power
Pertaining not to earth.   Passing her hand
Most lovingly over Sarah's tear-wet
Cheek, she queried with sympathetic voice
If she might not learn the cause of her grief ;
For well she knew it was not the pain that
Caused such bitter tears to fall mixed with the
Cry of " Mother ! O my mother ! "
'Mid broken sobs and tears the poor girl turned
To that dear friend in her distress, pouring
Out to her sympathetic ear the history
Of her grief and of her mother's sad and
Broken life.   " And now, to think that she is dead,
And I, her only child, cannot pay to
Her the last fond tribute of respect, seems
Almost more than I can bear ! " moaned Sarah
In her anguished grief.
" It is, in truth, a trial keen," replied
Sweet Cornie Houston.   " Perhaps 'twill soothe your
Grief to know I, too, have lost my mother.
With you, no pangs of remorse linger
Around your heart in memory of that
Dear and ever-cherished friend's decease :
While I must always bear the sting of self-
Reproach ; for 'twas through my own wilfulness
My mother was hastened to her death."

CHAPTER IX.

CORNIE'S STORY.

" WHEN I was sixteen, I, with an elder
        Sister, — who now stands in the place of a
Mother and a sister too, so kind is she
To me, — was sent away to school, and there
Formed the acquaintance of Ralph Hammond,
A young student of pleasing address. But
I since have learned his morals were corrupt.
Then I could in him no failing see, and
At last grew so infatuated, I
Was quite ready to accede to his proposed
Elopement, thinking it would be something,
Grand to relate in after-years : besides,
Would not the newspapers chronicle the
Event with superfluous items of their
Own ? Each Wednesday afternoon, the pupils,
From three to eight o'clock, had a holiday ;
The intervening hours to pass as best should
Suit their fancy. For several weeks, Ralph and
I the fondest love-letters had written
And exchanged, hiding them beneath a large
Flat stone at the end of the garden-walk.
Under cover of this impromptu office,
All our plans of elopement had been
Discussed and finally arranged ; and thus
The matter stood. I was to mingle with
4*

The others, careless and unconcerned, as
Though no weighty act was pressing on my
Heart.   The tea-bell rang at seven : and then,
Making an excuse, I hurried to my
Room, where I rapidly exchanged my dress
For the one I had selected ; hastily
Gathered a few most needful articles ;
Down the broad stairs sped, across the garden-
Walk, and out by the little wicket-gate,
Close by which Ralph was awaiting me.
' My darling girl ! ' he cried as he helped me
Through.   ' I was so afraid Maria would find
It out, and all our fun be stopped !
Now hurrah ! away for the station, or
We shall miss the train, and also miss
The boat.'   We were in time ; and quickly, and,
To my seeming, all too soon, we reached the
Station on the wharf ; for even then
My heart misgave me, and I wished myself
Back again by dear Maria, who, I knew,
Was ere this searching for Sister Cornie.

    " We safely reached New York ; were booked at the
Astor House.   Leaving me alone, Ralph went
Out to make inquiries relative to
A clergyman who would unite us.
He had been gone an hour or more, when on
My door there came a heavy knock.

    " Unthinking of the grief in store for me,
I answered the demand.   Before me stood
An official agent, bearing a telegram
From my sister, running thus : —
' Our mother is dead ! come home at once, dear
Cornie ! — MARIA.'

You, my dear Sarah, can imagine somewhat
Of my feelings in that hour. At once I
Started, and alone, leaving for Ralph a
Line, saying, ' Gone home. Farewell forever! —
CORNIE.'
In a state of mind bordering upon
Frenzy, I arrived at home, and found my
Sister's message was too true, and I had
Killed her!' "
  Powerful emotion shook Miss Houston's
Feeble form at the bare memory of
The dire calamity she had caused. Sarah
Gently urged her not to harrow up that
Sad past, as 'twould surely make her ill.
After a little, she resumed in calmer
Tones : —
  " Missing me at the supper-table, my
Sister ran up to our room to see what
Had become of me ; where, finding things in
Such disorder, she at once proceeded
To ' tidy up ' the room, as she expressed
It. Lifting from the floor the dress I'd worn,
With a gentle shake she was proceeding
To hang it in the wardrobe, when from its
Folds a letter fell, which she at once
Unclosed and read. And then she knew it all ;
For in that, the last one Ralph had written
Me, the plan of the elopement, and place
Of sojourn, was fully explained. At first,
My sister was bewildered ; but anon
She thought, ' I will not let our schoolmates know,
Since there is no need.' Speeding to the
Telegraph-room, she sent her message : —

' Cornie has eloped — New York — Astor House —
Tell me what to do. — MARIA.'

 " Our parents were seated upon the broad
Veranda of their country home, fronting
To the west; when down the tree-lined avenue
A horseman from the village galloped up,
And to our father gave Maria's despatch.
' Good God!' he, turning to mamma, cried out,
' Our Cornie has with some scamp eloped,
And gone to York! — so our Maria says.
Now, is not this a pretty ' — But the sentence
Was never completed; for mother was
Leaning against the trellis-frame of the
Door, white and motionless; and, in less time
Than it takes me to record it, *was dead!*
We all, for years, had known there was a small
Collection of water about her heart,
Which any undue excitement or grief
Would determine a rupture, producing
Almost instant death; and so we had
Always careful been heretofore. But then
My father was so surprised, he did not
Realize the danger his startling
News would engender. On me, and me
Alone, her sudden death must rest. At first,
I felt most wild with grief; but passing years
Have lifted from my heart its heaviest
Weights, crushing all joyousness from my life.
I find sweet consolation in the thought,
There is a purpose in each event of life:
A power divine is leading us through ways
We would not walk were we not guided there;

And what may now so strange and chanceful seem
Is but the hand of Fate, whose leading-lines
Are often tangled in the brittle web
Our hands *seem* weaving for ourselves, thinking,
Meantime, we our own destinies are shaping. "

CHAPTER XI.

THE TWO FRIENDS.

IN the quiet old town of N., bordering
Upon the lovely Connecticut, stands
A large, old-fashioned farm-house, shaded by
Elm-trees tall and old. Here Nathan Stevens
Had from his marriage lived, and his
Large family had been born and bred; and
Now all were gone save one, — the youngest son,
Who, at the time of which we speak, was
Not so very young, as more than thirty winters
Had set their seal upon his brow.
Mr. Stevens, or Uncle Nat as he
Was termed by old and young, was the brother
Of Sarah Horton's mother. He, on learning
Of the accident which had befallen
Her, wrote a letter overflowing
With sympathy and love. In it he begged
That Sarah would come to them as soon as
It was prudent, and make a lengthy stop.
The sorrowing girl was very glad when
She read Uncle Nathan's missive; for she had
Dreaded returning to her grandpa's,
Where every thing would so remind her of
Her mother. One thought, however, dampened
All her joy, — the idea of leaving
Cornie Houston, who was not able yet
To journey home. " If Cornie could but go

With her! And why not?" was Sarah's thought.
The new-born wish was set to words, to which
An answer came, — " Bring all the friends you wish:
Be sure they and you are welcome."
Thus it was, the week before Thanksgiving, —
That dear, time-honored day, — those two
So strangely brought together were resting
Beneath the ample roof of Uncle Nathan.
    Charles Stevens, though old enough in years,
Was a bashful man, wooing his books,
And not the ladies. His nature was
A sweet and silent one. Beneath his quiet
Ways were hidden rich veins of wit and
Knowledge, which sometimes, in unguarded
Moments, would peep out like sun-gleams beneath
A cloud. At first, of Cornie he was shy;
But after a time, as he grew wonted
To her presence, Sarah saw his eyes oft
Rest upon her friend with earnest gaze.
    Quietly and happily some six weeks
Had lapsed their record upon the book of Time,
When Cornie, upon receipt of home-letters,
Declared she must within the coming week
Bid adieu to her dear and cherished friends,
And turn her steps homeward. A friend
Of her father would pass that way within
Ten days, with whom she could journey all the
Way to her home. Not one word was uttered
In protest; and yet not one in the dear,
Familiar circle but felt it would be
A trial to lose the presence of this
Sweet girl, so patient and tender in all
Her ways.

" I'll tell you what, wife," good Uncle Nathan
Said, " we must make a party for these girls.
One good, old-fashioned time we'll have before
We part ; so Cornie here, in her Western
Home, may remember how we old farmers
Do things in Massachusetts."
    "Indeed we will ! " quoth Aunt Fannie.   " I'll send
To-morrow morn for Hannah Jenks, whose nose
Would be forever out of joint should there
Be a party gotten up, and she no
Finger in it.
I'm right glad you named it, Nathan ; for it
Is just what we need to rouse us up,"
Said Aunt Fannie, following him she loved,
To make arrangements for the gala-night.
    With the morning came Miss Hannah Jenks,
Who with her funny ways, and her " Massy sakes ! "
Kept the friends in a titter all the day.
Long before the festive hour arrived,
Every thing was pronounced by Aunt Fanny
And Hannah in " apple-pie order."
The lighter and more pleasing duties
Had fallen upon Charles and the two girls,
Who had ruthlessly robbed, not only Uncle
Nat's, but all the neighboring house-plants
Of their blooms, with which to deck the scene.
At last the eventful Thursday eve was
Welcomed by Uncle Nathan and his wife,
Who, dressed in their best, stood at the entrance
Of their large and brightly-lighted parlors,
Receiving the numerous and smiling
Guests fast assembling there.
The two friends, escorted by the bashful

Charles Stevens, were soon the cynosure of all
Eyes; though Sarah quickly perceived that 'twas
Her friend's sweet face and queenly grace of
Manner that was the centre of attraction.
No thought of jealousy wound itself into
Her heart, as is too often the case 'mid
Those professing warmest friendship.
She was an ardent admirer of Cornie
Herself, and would have felt aggrieved to see
That others did not share the loving homage
She laid with loyal love at her dear one's feet.
"I declare!" said Julia Alden, one of
The sprightly beauties of the town, "I didn't
Know before that your cousin *could* talk.
Just see him now, bending o'er Miss Houston,
Conversing as though his very life was
Forfeited!" Sarah turned her eyes upon
Her cousin's face, and saw what she before
Had only questioned in her mind might be
In the coming future. But how was it
With Cornie? She dared not ask, but would wait,
Giving them every chance for meeting, if
They wished.

Music was called for; and old Squire Hastings
With courteous smile and bow, begged Miss Houston
For a song, — "just one," he said.

With sweet assent she yielded, and was led
By the kind old gentleman to the
Piano; striking the keys of which, with
Gentle prelude she awakened into
Life the sympathetic cord running through
All hearts by the sweet melody of
Her impromptu song: —

5

"Dear friends, kind friends, of Massachusetts State,
My gratitude accept for favors small and great:
I came to you a stranger, ill, and quite forlorn;
And I can you repay with but a simple song.

When I'm far, far away, within my Western home,
I shall remember hours the brightest I have known.
My heart will linger oft 'mid scenes I love so well:
For we may meet no more; the future none can tell.

Life's changes, like a book, we're turning leaf by leaf;
For us our summer holidays are ever all too brief:
Soon the parting comes, when friendships true must sever;
But, oh, thank God! it cannot be forever."

Tears were in the eyes of the fair songstress
As she arose from the piano; and
Tears also filled the eyes of more than one
Honest heart who listened to the touching
Pathos of her song.
  The quiet stillness of the room was broken
By Uncle Nathan, who announced that "all
Those desirous of witnessing the tableaux
Would please adjourn to the library."
Approaching Cornie, he seemed to be pressing
Something upon her; to which, at first, she
Seemed disinclined to listen; but later
She bowed her head in acquiescence.
One of the young lady-actors had been
Suddenly called away; and there seemed
To be no one who could well fill her place,
Save Cornie; and thus was she selected.
The fifth scene represented her, queenly
And fair as the bridal rose, standing as
The betrothed of young Stevens, who, bending

On one knee, was in the act of placing
Upon her finger the betrothal ring;
When he whispered, "Look at me! oh, look!"
And she, with flushing cheeks, turned her eyes
For one brief moment on his face, and yet
Full long for her to read in his the old
Sweet story, so dear to the heart of woman
When coming, as it now did, from one
So well beloved.
"If this was only a reality!" he
Murmured, as the curtain folded them from
Sight. The grand and beautiful tableau,
"Rock of Ages," was the closing scene.
   Anon the merry company dispersed,
Writing down upon their calendar-
Book of "good times" another, and perhaps,
For some, a "last good time."

CHAPTER XI.

THE DEPARTURE.

THE bright beams of a winter sun streamed in
    Upon the thoughtful brow of Charles Stevens,
Who, seated in the pleasant library
Of his father's house, was seeking to still
His wildly-throbbing heart before the hour
Should come when he must bid farewell to one
Who had, for his peace of mind, become much
Too dear a treasure for him to lose, as now he
Saw he must, without a parting sigh.
While yet he sat buried in mental thought,
The door quietly unclosed, admitting
Cornie, who, smiling bade him a pleasant
Morn ; and had he seen her little book of
Songs? She could not find it elsewhere, so thought
It might have been mislaid among the books
In there.
" I'll help you search," said Charles, approaching near.
But when he found himself close by her side,
And thought how soon she would be gone, perhaps
Forever, his bashfulness slipped from him
Like a garment old, to be exchanged for
One newer and brighter. Seizing her hand,
Which he with gentle fervor pressed, he cried,
" How *can* I let you go, dear Cornie ?
The house will seem doubly desolate
Bereft of you and Sarah. I know not

How I ever lived before you came.
In truth, it was not living, but a tame
Existence, which the past few weeks have taught
Me most heartily to loathe.   By every
Pleasant hour we've passed, by all the sweet
Soul-thoughts between us nourished, by every
Song you've sung, by every joy we've shared
And thought us two between, I claim you for
My friend, near and dear.   And Cornie, darling!
Must it be *only* friend?   May not a nearer
Tie exist between us two? or is there
Some other who would claim the one *I* choose
For wife?"
Flushed with eagerness he stood, his hand
Upon her shoulder resting, awaiting
Her reply, which came at last, — "*It cannot
Be.*"
"No hope? — none? O Cornie! at least I may write?"
He queried with broken voice.   "It is not best;
But strive to forget me, as though we had
Never met," she answered back.
   Just then Sarah's voice was heard, loudly
Calling for her friend.   "I must go," Cornie
Gently said, looking up with wistful eyes,
As though she would daguerrotype
His face forever in her mind.   "Yes," he said,
Unconscious of the word; "and, as I go
This morn to F., you will be away ere
I return.   Perhaps 'tis better thus.
Sometimes remember him whose future days
Will ever be one memory of you.   And now
God bless you, and good-by!"
Silently Cornie Houston turned from him,
6*

Unheeding her fallen hankerchief as
She passed from the room.   Not so unmindful
He : for scarcely was she gone ere his eye
Rested upon it ; and, stooping, he raised
The dainty fabric to his lips again
And yet again, while the soft perfume
It distilled through all the room seemed redolent
Of her presence.   He placed it in his
Pocket in company with the book he
Had purloined.   Soon he, too, passed from the
Room, and anon was on his way to F.

Two hours more beheld Cornie and Sarah,
Accompanied by Uncle Nathan,
Driving toward the town of V. ;
For, at this junction, Cornie's father
Had written her she would meet his friend.
    Silence fell between the two so soon
To be separated.   Many sweet
Communings had knit their souls together
In close bonds of sympathy ; and now
God alone could know, if, in their coming
Years, their paths would ever mingle
Again as in the pleasant days agone.
    Arriving at the station, our party
Found there was none too much time, as the train
For the West was even then approaching.
Upon the platform of the advancing
Train stood a tall, dark-browed man, who, stepping
From the car ere yet it ceased to move,
Advanced towards the two, and asked
If either of the ladies was Miss
Houston, of whom he was to take charge
By request of her father.

Stepping forward, Cornie replied, " I
Am she you seek ; and you are Mr.
Golding ? These are my friends, — Miss Horton,
And her uncle Mr. Stevens."
At that moment, " All aboard !" sang out
The conductor's voice : so, with a hasty
Embrace, the two girls, with mutual vows
Of remembrance and correspondence,
Separated, — to meet how and where ?

Later that same day, Charles returned from his
Ride to F. in but a sorry plight.
" Beauty had taken flight," he said, " upon
His homeward way, at an ugly
Wheelbarrow standing by the wayside,
And began to run ; but he kept him
In check, until a sudden turn in
The road capsized the sleigh, throwing him
Upon the crusted snow, thereby
Bruising his face somewhat, and tearing
His coat, which he would be pleased to have
His cousin mend."
With a happy smile, she, procuring silk
And thimble, sat down by her cousin's
Side ; meanwhile telling him of Cornie
And her farewell words.
Turning the garment up and down, in
And in, there fell from its breast-pocket
A book and handkerchief, which needed
Not its sweet perfume to tell her who
Was once the owner. With furtive glance
She sought her cousin's face with
Questioning eyes. Seeing his

Desponding look, she asked with gentle
Voice, " What is it, Charlie dear, between
You two? Is it not to be ? "
" No; it is not to be," he answered back.
" But why ? " persisted Sarah.   " Did she
No reason to you assign ? "
" None."
" And yet," she mused, " I'm sure she loves
Him.   I'll solve the riddle yet."

CHAPTER XII.

A FEW days after Cornie's departure,
Sarah received from Madam R. a
Letter, offering for her acceptance the
Position of assistant teacher
In place of one who had left since her
Departure. A new lady principal
Was also installed; and various
Changes had transpired in the few weeks
Of her absence. Despite the urgent
Entreaties of her grandfather and
Uncle Nathan, Sarah wrote an eager
Letter of acceptance and thanks;
The time of her return appointed for
The coming week. Fondly and sadly
The young girl parted from those so dear
To her by ties of nature, and found
Herself once more a resident
Beneath the ample roof of Madam
R. She and the new principal were
To consort together, sharing one
Room, and, as events proved, many a
Pleasant hour of converse.
Glencora Mayo, from W., Vermont,
Was a lady gentle and prepossessing
In all her ways. Sarah at once felt
That they should be friends warm and true.

There was about her a nameless charm,
A quiet sadness, or serenity
Of peace that won upon each kind
Sympathy at once.   Not until long
Months afterwards did she learn the inner
Life of her friend; then, in the ravings
Of delirium, she unlocked from the
Closet of her heart the ghosts that had
For weary months been haunting her.
One name seemed ever upon her lips.
The most frantic appeals were made to
This same friend for love and protection.
One night, in the height of her mad ravings,
She seemed most determined to leave the
Room; while with gleaming eyes she whispered,
" I *must* see him : I *will* tell him
How all the time I loved but him ; and
How at last they told me, if I kept
Not my vow, my dead sister's curse would
Follow me and mine all our days ;
And, if I'd save him from reproach and
Sin, I must him renounce, e'en at the altar.
Oh hard and cruel fate !   Yet I was
Weak, and yielded to their power.
Now he has gone from me forever :
Another, a lady fair and gentle,
Is sheltered on the breast I love so well.
   " Another than Glencora
Fulfils the duties of a wife ; and
I, the faithless and yet the stricken
One, must bear the burden it seems
Ofttimes must crush my very soul."
For days and weeks did Sarah watch by

The sick-bed of her friend, allowing
None to share with her the lonely vigils
Of the night save the physician, who
Must necessarily understand
Far better than herself the electric
Sympathy between heart and brain.
She, in the reticence of her heart,
Felt that her friend's secret, which she so
Carefully guarded in her hours of
Health, should not be exposed to the oft
Careless and unsympathetic remarks
Of others. Though often weary, she
Still toiled on with tearful eye and aching
Brow ; and at last was rewarded one
Morning, during the doctor's daily
Visit, by hearing him say, " Your friend
Is better. Keep her perfectly quiet
When she awakens from this gentle
Sleep. I think I can trust you," he
Resumed : " for I give you this assurance,
That, under God, she owes her life to
You ; since the physician's efforts are
Futile unless seconded by the
Prompt, unceasing care you have
Displayed in following my directions,
Aside from the many little acts
The heart of a faithful nurse inspires.
Hereafter I recommend you to
Change your vocation of teacher to
That of nurse," he added with pleasant
Smile.
Some two hours later, as Sarah
Sat watching by her friend, now weak and

Helpless as a child, her eyes unclosed,
And, with a look of wonder, rested
Upon her attendant's face.　Gone, then,
Was the wild and burning look which
For many days had haunted them, and,
With a wistful gaze, they turned on surrounding
Objects.
With whispered voice she queried, "What is
It?　Why are you here?　Am I sick?
Why do things seem so strange to me?"
"Hush! you must not talk; but·be good, and
I will tell you all about it soon.
Now take this strengthening tea, and let
Me bathe your face.　There, now; that is nice.
You've been very ill, my dear, but now
Are out of danger."
The weary eyes soon closed again in
Slumber.　The next day, as Sarah was
Freshening up the room, Miss Mayo
Asked her with timid voice if she had
Talked in her sleep, and what she said.
With adroit tenderness, her friend told
Her of the fancies she had cherished,
And how that one name was ever on
Her lips; and that was Solon Gordon!
She told her how she saw from the first
Some heavy heart-grief was hidden
From the common gaze, as the miser
Hides his cherished gold; and so when she
Grew so ill, and unwittingly revealed
That which had long been hidden, she was
Determined in her mind none other than
Herself should listen to the ravings

Of her tortured mind : she had only
Done by her as she should wish a friend
To do by herself were she so circumstanced.
She had, she owned, learned so much of her
Friend's past, she would like to gather more
Some day, if in her friendship she could
Faithfully trust ; if not, no matter.
   What now she knew
Would sacred lie within her heart, and
She would ever feel the strongest
Sympathy and love for one who had
Bravely suffered so much and so long.

6

CHAPTER XIII.

"SOME years ago, I was the promised
Wife of my heart's dear and chosen one,—
Solon Gordon. My sister died, and,
Dying, wished me to promise some day
To marry her husband for the sake of
Her child. But passing time proved to
Me I could not with honor keep my
Vow. After the return of one I
Almost worshipped, whom I had driven
To exile for many months, I so
Far humbled my pride as to sue for
His forgiveness and a renewal
Of his love; to which his generous
Nature freely responded.
Another wedding-day was set; when
I, cowed and frightened by the jeering
Oaths and maledictions of those fiends
In human shape, again betrayed his
Confidence and love in me.
Not one word of palliation was
I permitted to offer to the
Being whom I had twice wantonly
Insulted through his tenderest feelings.
I suffered from an attack of brain-
Fever, which brought me so near Death's door,
It seems almost a wonder I did

Survive.   From that bed of anguish I
Arose to learn that the man I had
Twice outraged had gone, none knew whither.
Ere my strength had fully returned,
I was beset to marry Charles Steele.
Ah! he is rightly named.
I rebelled; and, incredible as
It may seem in these days, my brother
Kept me a prisoner in my room
For two weeks, and the last one served me
But one meal per day.   Opposition
To their will seemed so to enrage them,
They seemed more like brutes than human
Beings.   Finding at last that I would not
Yield to harsh treatment, they tried the
Persuasive; but again I was like
Adamant.   Too yielding in the past
To the will of others, I had learned
By bitter experience, when, as it
Seemed, almost too late, that my *heart* was
My best and most honest counsellor.
Finally I was turned from the house,
And forbidden ever again to
Darken it with my hateful presence.
I left it, all unknowing where my
Steps should lead, trusting the hand of God
Would guide and sustain me.
Feeling that I needed some active
And engrossing duty to divert
My mind from my own sorrows, I sought
A large city in the Empire State.
Soon after my arrival there, in
Answer to my application, I

Was elected assistant matron
In the Female Hospital. For four
Years I followed this life of toil and
Recompense: ay, recompense; for is it
Not such, when the weary faces of the
Sufferers light up with joy divine
At the approach of one who has toiled
To ease their pain, and soothe by kind
Ministrations their fretful repinings?
One sweet old lady, who in one year's
Time had been bereft of husband, child,
And home, won most upon my sympathies.
No doubt have I but her dear words of
Faith and trustful love in the Father's
Will did more to ease my heart than all
Else combined. So confident was she
Christ's power and love was over all
And in all; that what we needed most
We should receive, e'en though it should be
Farthest from our wills, — that I at
Last the same inculcated. The yoke I'd almost
Scorned to bear seemed lighter then, and I
Was not alone. The dear Lord was my
Helper and my friend: alone, deserted,
As I felt, I yet was not alone.
At last, it came to me my labor
There was done. The world was wide, and
Various occupations open to my
Acceptance. Always ardently
Fond of music, I bethought me of
A plan long ago cherished, — to be
A teacher of music. Perfecting
Myself in a method of recent .

Date, I threw myself once more upon
The world, a wanderer. · Another
Two years were passed in restless journeyings.
  "Through Massachusetts and New York I
Roamed. New Hampshire and Canada
My feet have also pressed. I loved my task.
  "O music! grand and sublime art thou
In thy native power! What human
Heart so dull and dead that thy sweet voice
Cannot awaken to holy
Symphony? Thrills of rapture keen seem
To chase the life-blood from my heart when
The soft music of Handel and Mozart
Floods the air with its rhythmic melody.

  "And yet again I wearied of my
Wanderings. Casually I saw the
Advertisement of Madam R., and
Hither came, unknowing how long my
Wild unrest will slumber. Here *we* have
Met, the corner-stone of our friendship
Placing upon sympathy of soul.
Many ties of friendship have I formed
Since my banishment from kindred friends ;
But none have proven sweeter than yours.
Oh, may this blessed bond, so sweet and
Pure and so true, grow strong, and yet more
Strong, with passing years! Yet, despite
These friendships, I often query of
My soul, What good do I do, or what
Happiness confer? My days seem but
A continuance, or like some
Divided mechanism of art,

6*

That keeps perpetual motion because
It cannot stop save at the master
Touch.   I find no consolation
Where'er I turn.   Upon a pedestal
High I have placed Duty, dressed in sombre
Robes.   Do as I will, she mocks me.
While crowning her with my hardly-won
Labors, she wreaths for my gaze Love's
Fairest pictures.   A home she shadows forth,
A perfect garden of contented love,
Where Hope and Peace walk hand in hand,
Where Joy blooms eternal, and Faith dies
Not, — a very paradise on earth.
   " But for Duty, stern and pitiless
As Death, this bower of Eden might
Have sheltered me, and all my days been
Crowned with Peace."

CHAPTER XIV.

RECREATION.

THE seasons sped their annual rounds, —
Summer succeeding winter, and winter
Summer. Sarah Horton, after an
Absence of years, was spending her few
Vacation-weeks with Uncle Nathan
And Aunt Fannie. Glencora Mayo,
Too, had been invited, but gently
Declined, feeling that duty compelled
Her to remain at the seminary,
As some of the pupils were obliged
To pass the short reprieve from study
In the quiet old town, and still more
Quiet institute.

Sarah was greeted by her cousin
Charles in his usual friendly
Manner; and yet there was an added
Something, that gave him a new interest
In her eyes.

The second morn after her arrival,
While busily engaged with Aunt Fan,
Her cousin came in, inquiring " if
She would not enjoy a visit to
The Old Hermit of the Mountain.
There is a party going from here ;
Will start in just an hour. And, mother,
Please to see we have a lunch prepared."

At the hour appointed, the pleasure-
Seekers all faced the mountain.
During the drive, Charles Stevens oft
Questioned his cousin respecting Miss
Houston.   With manner unconcerned,
She told him of her friend's past life ;
Of her morbid feeling in respect
To love, and the reason thereof.
" I know," said Sarah, " she cares for you
As you desire ; but, feeling as she
Does, it was her own wild caprice that
Caused her mother's death, she deems the vow
Then made — henceforth to have with love no
More to do — still binding : and so, though
Loving you with affection strong and
Pure, she will herself deny, without
Confiding the same to you. or even
Hinting of her heart's fond devotion ;
Fearing, as well she may, that your
Solicitations, combined with the pleadings
Of her own woman's heart, would break down
The wall of reserve behind which she
Stands intrenched.
If," added Sarah, " I did not deem
Her Quixotic, and suffering from
Her own resolve, I'd not have told you,
Cousin mine.
Of course you've heard the adage old,
' Faint heart ne'er won fair lady ; ' which same
I advise you to remember, you
Dear, good, bashful coz ! ' "
    Anon the party, leaving their horses
Some rods below, were toiling up

The shelving rocks to the Hermit's Cave,
Which they soon reached; finding that, early
As they had started, two separate
Parties had them preceded.

It was, in truth, a primitive style
Of living, though not quite a hermit's
Life, judging from the names recorded
In the "guest-book" lying there.
Our party, standing and sitting about
In various groups as best their fancy
Suited, were soon joined by two young men,
And seeming strangers to all there present.
Approaching Sarah and her cousin,
The taller of the two, lifting his
Hat, bowed low, begging to know if he
Had not the honor of addressing
Miss Horton, the sometime ardent friend
Of Miss Cornie Houston.

" I see my face you do not recognize:
And 'tis not strange, as you had but a
Passing glimpse, when your thoughts were all
Engrossed in parting from your friend: so
I must be my own re-introducer.
I am Mr. Golding, your friend's former
Escort; and this gentleman is Mr.
Hubbard, — Miss Houston's cousin, and my
Dear college-chum."

Mutual greetings being exchanged,
The four, thus brought in contact, were soon
Engaged in lively and earnest talk.
Many questions fell from Sarah's lips
Respecting her friend, which both young men
Seemed eager to answer; while Charles, with

Love-quickened sense, caught every word
While talking with seeming interest
With the friend or cousin, as the case
Might be. Harry Golding seemed most persistent
In his endeavors to please Miss Sarah ;
So much so, that the lookers-on
Began to make comments at his expense.

During the hours of rambling, and
Afterward the dinner-picnic, shared
By all, the two strangers were introduced
To the rest of the party from N.
Miss Julia Alden declared at once,
She should set her cap for Mr. Hubbard,
For two reasons : viz., because he was
The cousin of that darling Miss Houston ;
And he also seemed in her eyes much
The nicer of the two. She did not
Favor tall men : they were apt to be
Conceited.

Doll Hubbard, who, notwithstanding Miss
Julia's assertion, was as conceited
As the generality of men, soon saw
His name was written down among the
List in Miss Alden's good graces : and,
To assure her of her good taste, he
Certainly exerted himself to please
The wilful lady ; and, as ofttimes
It proves, in pleasing her he found he
Yet more pleased himself.

The lengthening shadows of the bright
Afternoon sun warned the picnickers
That it was time to leave the mountain
Wilds, as they had yet a long ride before

Them.   By invitation of Charlie
Stevens, the two young men, so lately
Strangers, were induced to make a
Visit to N., and stop, meanwhile, at
Uncle Nathan's.
    While they were waiting for the teams,
Hal Golding said to Sarah, " You will
Please ride with me, and Doll with your
Cousin." — " Ah, indeed! it is immaterial
To me."   Which answer caused Mr.
Golding to gnaw his nether lip in
A fashion quite his own.
He thought, " Where is the girl's mind?   I don't
Believe she even knows if I am
Dark or fair, old or young.   I'm not used
To such cool treatment from ladies ; and
I'll teach her the lesson not to treat
Me with such cool indifference ! "

CHAPTER XV.

VISIONS.

THE two weeks following were rife with each
   Pleasure the country could afford.
Picnics of every description, long
Boat-rides on the beautiful Connecticut,
Re-unions at different homes, pleasant
Walks and talks, no more to be indulged:
For soon the happy company of
Friends would be scattered, to meet no more;
Or, if they met some day in the future,
They would not be the same as then.
New scenes, new ties, the world's hard buffets,
Would change produce; and though glad to meet,
And often longing for another grasp
Of the old friend's hand, yet when clasped, and
Eyes gazed once again in those so dearly
Loved, *a change is there.* What is it?
We see it, we feel it, although their
Words and acts may be as kind as in
The past.
No more the tender eyes beam the same;
No more the smiling lips sing the sweet refrain
   They sang bright years agone.
There is a something lost, we scarce know what:
When friends long parted meet again, they've not
   The freshness of their morn.
Ah, Change! twin-sister of old Time art thou.
We must yield thee homage, unto thee bow,

Laying life's sweet hopes down.
In vain we'd hold thee back ; thou wilt not stay :
Joys our hearts find most complete soon fade away,
    And for our past weave a crown.
                            One more
Day of pleasure yet remained ; and it
Was finally decided in the glen
To have a rural picnic.   Sarah
And her cousin were hostess and host,
All needful preparations making.
No shadow marred the beauty of the
Sky, and no cloud hovered o'er
The pleasure-seekers, on this last gala-
Day, save sometimes the thought of coming
Separation.   Harry Golding proved
Sarah's shadow, much to her annoyance.
Him she avoided much as was
Consistent with her character of
Hostess, not wishing to pain him by
A refusal of the honor he
Designed for her ; for, woman-like,
She read his heart's true wish.
Fate and Harry Golding willed otherwise.
    Somewhat apart from the others she
Sat, wearied with her unusual efforts
To entertain so many guests ;
When Golding, seeing her thus alone,
And somewhat sad, approached, and at her
Feet himself he threw with happy smile.
" At last," he said, " I see you as I
Wish, — alone.
To-morrow, as you know, our pleasant
Party of five-weeks' duration must
                7

Separate, and all these happy hours
Be numbered with the past.
I came here seeking pleasure, and the boon
Has been granted me beyond my hopes ;
Although my heart I can but question
How much has your dear presence enhanced
My pleasure.   From our first brief meeting
At the station, my thoughts to you have
Oft reverted.   Miss Cornie, who has
Your picture, oft laughed at me because
I asked so many, and, to her seeming,
Useless questions respecting you ;
Oft with this assertion ending,
' That girl shall be my wife, if she will
Me accept.'
From Cornie I have learned of your early
Trials, of your lonely life, bereft
Of home and parents as you are, and
Yet surrounded by friends kind and true.
   " With my hand, which I now offer you,
Wealth and high position you'll receive.
No more this hand " — pressing the one he
Had in his ardor taken — " shall toil
To gain such pittance small.   Instead,
A lady you shall be, and loving
Mistress of my heart."
   " Am I really less a lady
That I now earn my daily bread ?
No, Harry Golding: your wife I'll never
Be.   The life of toil you've pictured forth
Better far suits me than the idle
One you'd woo me to.
We all from the Creator's hand first

Fare alike. The accidents of wealth
And distinction in my eyes are nought.
Forgive me if I press too sorely
On your pride by pointing you to the
Many paths open to you and honor.
Go, toil and win your way amid the
Toiling great ones of the day. Set high
Your mark, and guard with jealous care.
What! you, a man, strong and young, with wealth
At your command, would idly fritter
The God-given years in senseless rounds
Of pleasure? O Harry Golding! I
Do beseech of you to pause ere yet
Too late. Remember, this life's brief span
Is soon run out: and much it does
Behoove each one of us to fill our
Record-book with deeds of virtue;
For, when comes the reckoning-day, what
Then will matter the fashion of our
Garments here? That will not be recorded;
But the good deeds done, the one soul saved,
Some heavy yoke lightened, — *these* will upon
The Book of Life be written with our
Names. Oh! is it not worth striving for,
Toiling for, and, if need be, dying for?"
    Sarah's face, beautiful with the soul's
Reflections, was raised in earnestness
To her companion's gaze; and he, more than
Ever infatuated with her, because
Of her reticence and coolness to
Himself, determined to make yet one
More appeal for her love.
    "If," said he, "I prove to you and others

I am with the tide a co-worker,
And bind upon my brow the laurel-
Wreath of fame, *then* may I not be
Rewarded with your love, to me the
Highest honor that I crave?"
  " Do not ask it," she replied with voice
Low and sad. " We ne'er should be congenial.
No *true* soul-sympathy exists
Between we two. And forgive me, but
I think much of your present sorrow
Lies in your thwarted wish. To will is,
With you, to have; but it may not always
So remain. 'Tis for yourself, without
Regard to me, I'd have you change.
You'll find 'twill bring you sweet content
If you will yourself ofttimes deny,
And thereby upon some other less
Favored one a cheering hope bestow.
  " You will some day thank me," she resumed,
" That I can better understand your
Needs than does yourself; and this is but
A passing shadow athwart your life.
Accept my earnest friendship, and be
Assured your future path will a recipient
Be of my friendly hopes and earnest
Prayers."

CHAPTER XVI.

REWARDED.

BY earnest request of his late guests,
   Charles was to accompany them, first
On a trip to the White Mountains ; then
To Saratoga and Lake George ; later,
To their home in the West.
   Doll Hubbard was in the highest spirits ;
For he would have the bright, piquant Miss
Julia for his own some day in the
Future.   They both were young as yet, and
Her parents would not listen to her
Marriage for some years at least.
   Sarah and Golding parted as friends
Ordinarily part, with pleasant
Wishes for each other, and full-spoken
Words of remembrance.   " Give me some
Souvenir of these pleasant hours ! " he
Cried, when standing in the hall but a
Moment preceding his farewell.
   " And shall you them forget ?
Howe'er, I give you *this ;* and let
It ring in your heart its pæans sweet.
May it be your honored mistress, the
Companion of every secret thought,
The idol of your manhood strong, the
Recompenser of your age ! — Excelsior ! "

At last they were gone ; and the old home
Of Nathan Stevens seemed so quiet
And forsaken, our friend felt almost
Glad when the hour of her departure
Arrived. Ere she returned to H., she
Was to pay her grandpa a few days'
Visit ; for much she wished, yet dreaded,
To see her mother's grave. That act of
Love and duty accomplished, she returned
Again to Madam R.'s, where she was
Joyfully received by teachers and
Pupils, but by none so truly and
Fondly welcomed as by Glencora,
Who had suffered from her friend's absence
More perhaps than she would to herself
Have owned. The same old routine was
Renewed, and Sarah felt herself *at home.*
Sometimes a smile of conscious pleasure
Her lips would cross, in memory of
Harry Golding's blank dismay, when he
Realized that she, even she, the
Poor orphan-girl, with no inheritance
Save her brains, had dared to refuse his
Proffered hand, preferring her life of
Toil to the drudgery of his love.
Of Glencora she a confidante made,
Who much approved her choice. Together
They would talk and plan of coming years,
When they, with more experience, should
Themselves be founders of a school that
Must always for its motto bear
" Excelsior ! "

Occasionally Sarah from her cousin
Heard; and in the last he wrote,
" Next week, cousin mine, we are *en route*
For Rock Island ; and soon I shall clasp
In mine the hand of the dearest and
Most lovable of created beings.
Wish me joy; wish me success! Did I
Not know how much your sympathies
With me were cast, I'd not thus freely
Speak: and, when I my fate shall learn,
I'll let you know; for from what yourself
Has said, and what from her friends I glean,
I shall not take her former ' No ' as
Final answer."
    A few weeks later, and Cornie Houston
Penned the following letter to her
Friend: " My darling friend, and sometime cousin,
Yourself prepare for a missive long,
And perhaps wearisome ; and yet I
Can but feel your sympathetic heart
Will truly rejoice that at last I
Saw the foolishness of my vow,
And so abjured it.
As you may guess, I was surprised and
Glad when once again I looked upon
My dear beloved's face. Mine I know
Was of a scarlet flame, when, bending
Low, he said, ' Dear Cornie! was I wrong
To come ?' — ' Not wrong, but right,' I answered
Back ; and then the joyful pressure of
His hands set all my pulses throbbing.
Two blissful hours we passed in happy
Interchange of thought. To him I then

Confessed my youthful folly and its
Sad consequence, causing me to make
That bitter vow, which, made, I felt in
Honor bound to keep, till o'er-persuaded
By reason and his love. He argued,
That, in addition to the past error,
I was, in refusing him when loving
Him, doing a far greater wrong than
E'er before; for were not two lives
Blighted instead of one?

   " I had, by my hours of anguish,
Expiated the result of that mad freak,
And now surely had earned the boon of
Love.

   " I had so thirsted for a sight of
His dear face, I could not struggle long
Against the pleading voice and my own
Fond heart. But, when he pressed for an
Early marriage, I could not yield assent.
' Not yet, oh! not yet; give me time,' I
Urged. ' We can wait: we're not old or
Gray.' — ' But why?' said he. ' Life at the longest
Is but short; and I have lived so alone,
It seems I cannot you resign, when
At last you own your heart is mine.
My darling! let me claim you this fall:
Let me not return alone to pass
In exile another dreary winter.'

   " His entreaties I firmly resisted;
Finally promising, that when the
Next September sun should tint with warm
Radiance fair scenes of Titian hue,
Then would I become his bride. With kiss

Like morning dew, we the compact sealed;
And then, ourselves bethinking that there
Were others than we two upon the
Sphere terrestrial, we joined our friends.
To me, dear Sarah, it was indeed
The happiest evening of my life.
Song after song we sang, while o'er the
Keys my fingers ran with gleeful touch.
   " 'There is a song just out,' friend Harry
Golding said, ' which I incline to think
All our hearts will suit just now.'
   " As we that happy evening closed with
That sweet song, so I will my letter end
By giving you the same, hoping you
May some day not far distant apply
It for yourself: —

" Ever on my lips, like unbreathed prayer,
  Thy name is wafted on the balmy air:
  There is no time or spot, afar or near,
  But *thou* art remembered with smile or tear

" At the morning's dawn, and at the éven-tide,
  My soul is walking ever by thy side:
  My yearning heart cries out to thee in vain,
  Breathing but tender prayers born of pain.

" The past has garnered such memories kind,
  And close about my heart an altar twined:
  The present, too, has mingled joy and pain,
  The future unkind words shall never stain.

" When that hour comes which to all will not fail,
  When my soul goes forth with the boatman pale,

When Death's cold icy hand shall chill my brow,
My prayer then shall be the same as now.

" First and last, dearest and best,
  Thy name shall with me float to dreamless rest:
  E'en in the grave, with that I'm not alone ;
  For me 'tis heaven, rest, and home.

" Ever your   " CORNIE."

CHAPTER XVII.

AT LAST.

ANOTHER year, freighted with mortality's
    Joys and sorrows, had circled on her
Way since last we looked on Sarah, who
Now, in company with Glencora,
Was passing vacation-weeks at Uncle
Nat's. Within the year her grandpa had
Passed on, and the dear old home to the
Hand of strangers had fallen ; for his
Two maiden sisters long ago had
Returned to Mother Earth their tribute.
With happy zeal did Sarah's fingers
Deftly fashion the pretty garments
Destined for herself and her friend, who
No aptitude possessed for tiny
Items of a lady's stylish dress.
    And why was Sarah thus anxious for
The adornment of her friend and self?
Simply in honor of her cousin's
Alliance with her almost worshipped
Friend, dear Cornie Houston.
She, and her later chum Miss Mayo,
Were bidden to the wedding, but could
Not well accept, and compromised the
Warm entreaties of their friends with the
Assurance of meeting the bridal

Party at Saratoga when they
Should there arrive. Much need had Sarah
For her haste, as time was passing on ;
And, in a letter late received, she
Learned that the tourists, per New York,
Would reach " Fashion's Babel " the coming
Week.

   So in and out among the fabrics
Fine her needle flew, until at last
All was complete, and nicely packed in
Trunks fitted with compartments neat.
It was a blissful treat to the two
Weary girls for a time to leave all
Care behind, and revel in Nature's
Panorama, so pleasing to the eye.

   The bright September day to its close
Was drawing, when the two girls, somewhat
Weary with their long and dusty ride,
First pressed the platform of the dépôt
Small and old. No friendly face was there
To give them welcome, save the hackmen,
Who with their usual gusto bawled out,
" A carriage, marm?" " Congress Hall?" " Union?"
  " Clarendon ? " " Columbian ? " " Pavilion ? " " New
      York ? "
" Carriage to the American House " was
Indeed an announcement pleasing to
The bewildered girls, as 'twas there Sarah
Had been directed by her cousin to
Go, and there their pleasant rooms had for
Weeks been engaged.
The bridal party had not arrived :
So from their room they did not venture,

Save to partake of their simple tea.
Ere yet the rosy beams of old Sol
Threw his brightning rays across the
Slumbrous town, the country-bred girls
Were out drinking in the morning air,
Permeated with the attributes of
The many springs, the waters of which
They did not at first over-fancy.
Returning from their long and appetizing
Walk, joyfully were they surprised to
Find their party already domiciled.
　With eager joy, Sarah rushed up the
Stairs leading to her cousin's parlor.
More quietly, Glencora followed.
" O my darling Cornie Houston ! " cried
Sarah : " do I indeed behold your
Dear, sweet face ? " kissing lips, cheek, and brow
Ere her friend could respond save by her
Kisses fond.　Charles, approaching, said, " I
See, ' mad-cap ' cousin mine, I must your
Memory refresh, and to you
Introduce *my wife*, and your cousin,
Mrs. Charles Stevens."
　" What a jealous bundle of masculinity
He's got to be ! now, hasn't he, my
Darling one ?　Oh ! pray forgive me for
My remissness in introducing
To your kind regard my cherished
Glencora Mayo."　Saying which, she
Turned toward her friend, who, reclining
In the large rocker, seemed Parian
Marble, so white and still was she.
To their inquiries kind, and efforts

8

For relief, she begged them no alarm
To feel, since 'twas nothing but a pain
In her heart, from which she had of late
Felt more free until that morn ; and, as
Quiet would soonest her restore, by
Their leave she would retire, and join them
Later in the day.
   Sarah, who accompanied her to
Their room, was startled by the thrilling
Pathos of her voice, as the words, half
Breathed, fell from her lips, "I've seen him, — *him*, —
Gordon ! Did you not see that man, tall
And dark, yet, oh ! so beautiful, pass
Down the hall as we entered ? "
   " Indeed, no : I no one saw but you ;
And think you must have been mistaken.
One's fancy, you know, sometimes strange freaks
Will play. Some one, perchance, there was, who
Much resembles this friend so cherished :
It could not well be him, you know."
   The gong was sounded ; and Sarah, by
Entreaty of Glencora, left her alone,
While she with her friends proceeded to
The ample dining-room. Cornie's
Sister and husband, General Davidson,
Escorted the newly-married pair ;
And Sarah, by her cousin, was then
Presented to the Reverend Mr.
Gordon, and by whose side she sat in
Bewildered thought. " Glencora was right.
After all," she mused : " but how came he
Here? and how so intimate as he
Seems with Cornie and her friends ? " So much

She speculated with regard to
Him, her appetite, which she had thought
So keen, seemed to utterly have fled.

  Soon as by courtesy allowed, she
Her cousin questioned respecting the
" Divine," and learned that he, being an
Old college-chum of Davidson, was
By the latter invited to unite
The newly-wedded ones, and afterwards
To join their party in a pleasure-
Trip. " The poor man," continued Cornie,
" Has seen ' piles of trouble ; ' and, though so
Youthful in his looks, is now a
Widower, with two young lads, his sons.

  " Dear Sarah, I am *so* happy ! " whispered
The blushing bride ; " and I wish others
To be as blest ; though not many *can*
Be quite as much so as myself,"
Glancing toward her husband with love-
Freighted eyes : " and so I have been
Thinking how nice 'twould be if you would
Only show your better self to this
Good yet sorrowful man. In his
Early youth he was most shamefully
Used by one who him professed to love,
Yet who *twice* his confidence betrayed.
Exiled from his former home, he most
Hastily united with one who
Proved indeed a fitting wife and friend,
But whom it was not his fortune long
To possess. Death, the all-conquering,
Bore her to the land of shadows :
There his twin-children have also gone.

His property he lost by fire not
Long ago. His health is also broken.
Ah! why is it some must bear a yoke
So heavy, and others one of flowers?
Pity," added Cornie, " they say, is
Akin to love : if so, I'm sure you
Him will love, since pity him you must."

CHAPTER XVIII.

FATE.

"IT surely *is* Fate," mused Sarah, as
 She her way wended to the room where
She by Glencora's request left her,
And whom she now found enjoying a
Restful sleep. Quietly she darkened
The room, and, herself by the window
Sitting, mused of Life's strange crossings, which
Surely was not *all chance ;* else why were
These two, so long and strangely divided,
Brought in contact without foreknowledge
Of the other ? And, as Fate seemed most
Earnestly inclined to solve the riddle
Of their past, no human hand should
Interfere ; at least, not her's. Anon
There came on the door a gentle rap ;
And Cornie, radiant with happiness,
Upon the threshold stood, and, with voice
Attuned to the quiet room, questioned
Sarah of her friend. Learning of her
Sleep, she begged her cousin to prepare for
A drive to the "Spouting Spring," called one
Of Nature's curiosities ; said to have
Been discovered by prophecy of
A dream, or spirit-warning. "We shall
8*

With us take a lunch," continued Cornie,
" As we may be away some hours."
   Leaving for the sleeper a note
Explanatory of her absence, she
Speedily joined the party below,
And anon was, with the rest,
Complaining of the dust, and the land
So dry and barren.   Somewhat amused
Was Sarah at Cornie's finesse in
Bringing between her clerical friend
And herself a pleasant interchange
Of thought, combined with friendly acts of
Courtesy; which Gordon, being a
Gentleman in all his ways, was not
Slow to offer, and which Miss Sarah
Accepted in the same kind spirit.
   Having lunched, and tested the flavor
Of the " Sulphur " as well as the " Spouting "
Spring, our party to the " Glass Factory "
Journeyed.   A pleasant hour was consumed
In watching the operators at their
Labor, and in gathering trophies
Of their visit, a less fortunate
One some day to regale with said
Exhibitions.   Deciding at last nothing
Else was worth their notice, they homeward
Turned.   On Circular Street they paused by
Gordon's request ; and there he left them,
His footsteps turning toward the Park,
The others passing on to the " Empire "
And " High-Rock" Springs; then home, per Broadway.
North.

Glencora from her long-refreshing
Sleep arose.   Soon Miss Sarah's note
Caught her eye.   "Ah! so they've gone," said she.
" I'm truly glad; for now I can a
Few more hours of quiet have in which
My heart to fortify against the
Shock this morn received at sight of that
Once-familiar form so like to him :
And yet himself it could not be ; for
He is far from here, and married too.
O heart ! poor foolish thing, to flutter
Thus in memory of one who has
Ere this forgotten thee !' " Soliloquizing
Thus, Glencora herself arrayed in
A black grenadine, with wheat-ears
Sprinkled o'er it ; corsage low, and her round
White arms gleaming through the texture thin
Like things of wax.   Amid her tresses
Loosely flowing she twined a spray of
Natural flowers.   Thus simply yet,
Tastefully adorned, she slowly and lone
Down Broadway passed, uncertain where her steps
Would lead ; until, feeling the need of
The cool, refreshing water, the Park
She entered, and liberally she quaffed
From the " Columbian."   Upon the
Upper walk of " Congress Park " she sat,
Deadened to every outward scene, but
Keenly alive to Memory's touch.
Sitting thus, with eyes upon the earth
Intent, and soul-visions of the past
Absorbing all her mind, she noticed
Not the manly step so near, pausing

At last in front of her, while a ne'er-to-
Be-forgotten voice questioned thus : —
  " Do I indeed behold her who once
Bore the name Glencora Mayo ? or
Is this of the brain some fancy ? Yes,
You are, you must be, Glencora !
Oh ! what strange fate brings you here, to mock
Me once again with the witchery
Of your love, so sweet, and yet so fickle ?
Methought my heart had learned its lesson
Of forgetfulness ; when, lo ! one glimpse
Of your dear face divests it of its
Boughten robe, leaving it bare and stricken.
Glencora ! O Glencora Mayo !
Would that I had ne'er beheld you, lovely
As you are ! for you have blighted the
Freshness of my youth, tarnished my dreams
Of power, and despoiled my future :
And yet — oh, madness of despair ! — I
Love you ; ay, adore you ! "

  With changing cheek Glencora listened
To his words ; and, though his tones of love
Thrilled all her heart, she thought of his wife,
Whom his present words to her thus had
Outraged. With tear-filled eyes she turned to
Him, saying, " I *once* thought Solon Gordon
The prince of honor. I now see my
Mistake ; since no true man would venture
Thus to speak. It matters not what our
Relations in the past have been : the
Present should be remembered, and *your wife*."

" My wife is now an angel there," said
Gordon, turning his eyes so sorrowful
Toward heaven. " I have no wife, no
Home, no friend I almost said : but that
I have no right to say, since Jesus
Bears for me my crown ; which I shall
Some day wear, if I do but faithful keep."

" Forgive me !" and Glencora's hand once
More upon that strong arm rested. " Sit
By me," — moving along, — " and tell me
Of your past since last we met ; then, if
You wish, the favor I'll return."

Hours passed on ; and they two, by Fate
Separated, and by the same power
Re-united, still talked of past, present,
And future.

Returning from their drive, Sarah hastened
Glencora to find ; and whom, not
Finding, she searched for far and near.
At last, some premonition warned her
That all was well with her, and not to
More disturbance make. Alone she
Sauntered toward the Park, which almost
Seemed deserted in the hush of coming ·
Twilight. At last, sitting upon a
Double seat, Sarah saw her friend ; and,
As she had divined, her companion
Was the restless Gordon.
They, so engrossed by each other, did
Not hear the intruding step drawing
Near and nearer, until at last she
Could but hear the sweet words of her friend,
Who, with head upon his shoulder resting,

His arm about her thrown, thus breathed of
Her soul's sweet content : —

    " The light is fading down the sky ;
      The shadows grow and multiply ;
        I hear the birdies' evening song :
        But I have borne with toil and wrong
          So long ! — so long !
      Dim dreams my drowsy senses drown :
      So, darling ! kiss my eyelids down.

    " My life's brief spring went wasted by ;
      My summer's ended fruitlessly ;
        I learned to hunger, strive, and wait :
        I found you, love, — oh happy fate !
          So late ! — so late !
      Now all my fields are turning brown :
      So, darling ! kiss my eyelids down.

    " Oh blessed hour ! oh perfect rest !
      Thus pillowed on your faithful breast :
        Nor life nor death is wholly drear,
        O tender heart ! since you are here,
          So dear ! — so dear !
      Sweet love ! my soul's sufficient crown :
      Now, darling ! kiss my eyelids down."

CHAPTER XIX.

STELLA GRAHAM.

THE day following the one of so
 Many happy incidents, a ride
To the lake was proposed; and to which
All most happily concurred, save one, —
Miss Sarah, who declared she could not
Go, as she had home-letters that must
Be written: besides, if she went, an
Odd number would be formed, which she quite
Solemnly averred would be fatal
To their pleasure. They finally were
Persuaded, and left her to her own
Devices. Her letters being done,
She started on an aimless stroll
About the lovely village. Passing
Caroline Street, she, from a rustic
Cottage near, heard such heaven-born strains
Of music as held her an enchanted
Listener. A sweet girlish voice oft
Broke forth in song like some bird beating
Its fettered wings against its prison-
Cage; and in those notes was breathed a heart's
Crushed sorrow. Unconsciously Sarah
Against the fence-railing leaned, drinking
In with eager ear the notes of harmony.
Some little time she thus stood, unheeding
The passers-by, who rudely jostled;

Feeling but one wish just then ; viz.,
To know who had invoked such music
Almost divine. Anon her attitude
From the house was noticed : from whence a
Lady grand and beautiful, although
Her hair was snowy white, in the open
Door-way stood, and questioned Sarah
If she felt ill; else why did she upon
Their yard-fence lean ? No queen could be more
Fair, no voice more pleasing to the ear,
Than was this dear old lady's, whose eyes
Were yet as blue and kind as in her
Early youth, whose cheek still bore the rose's
Bloom, and whose mouth itself was sweetness.
So thought our heroine as she looked on
Her; and born in a moment was the
Wish to know and have her for a friend.
Sarah most truly felt alone since
Glencora had returned to him so long
Beloved. She knew for her friend she felt
Rejoiced; and yet a pang 'twould bring
Despite of all to see how quickly
Cornie and Glencora both had her
Forsaken for the love of man. She
The same would do, no doubt, if ever
She loved; and more than foolish it seemed
To give it a passing thought. They all
Loved her well, and much would laugh at her
Sad fancies.
    " Will you allow me to come in and
Rest, dear madam ? " questioned Sarah. " I
Feel a little weary, and homesick
Withal." — " Certainly, dear child," the kind

Old lady said. " You do look tired and
White.   Let me take your hat and gloves ; and
Rest you in this chair," — drawing forth a
Large stuffed rocker, which to her guest's eye
Seemed most inviting.
   The room in which she sat was to her
Vision like some fairy picture, sweet
And beautiful.   Upon the floor was spread
A carpet of white ground, with bouquets
Of lovely flowers sprinkled o'er it.
A marble-topped table stood in the
Centre of the floor, upon which was
A rich vase of Bohemian ware filled
With the late autumn flowers.   A what-not,
Laden with many a curious
And tasteful relic, one corner filled.
A pretty tête-à-tête was rolled against
The wall.   A parlor-organ and
Piano also graced opposite
Sides of the room.   Ottomans of rich
Embroidery mixed among the stately
Chairs.   One of Rubens' paintings hung
Against the walls, and others of less
Note.   Brackets of every size and shape
Were scattered here and there, all laden
With trifling gems of art.   Over-
Head a pretty bird-cage hung, in which
Dick and Charlie kept house year after
Year, and, when fancy willed, free concerts gave.
The long white curtains were of lace, and
Just revealed the pretty shades beneath.
Upon a bracket shaped for books, a
Fine assortment met the eye: all the best

9

Literature of the day was gathered
There. A stand close by was laden
With fruit of various kind ; but the
Fairest thing of all was the young girl
Reclining upon a couch, close drawn
To the open window. All other
Items Sarah's eye had taken at
A glance, save this sweet statue ; for such
She seemed. Scarce eighteen summers their seal
Had set ere Death his signal gave, and,
By his cruel frown, the coming years
Affrighted. Her brow was broad, full, and ·
High, with eyebrows arching over eyes
Of darkest hue, yet full and soft as
Midsummer's dream ; nose slightly aquiline ;
Pure oval cheeks, compressing a mouth
Broad and sweet with human richness ;
Chin perfect in its outline,
Upon a neck slender, yet graceful, the lovely
Head was poised, with its wealth of shining
Hair ; her perfect form was but a child's
In stature ; her hands, idly resting
In her lap, were beautiful beyond
Compare.

    Sarah thought of the " Arabian Nights "
And its enchanted land ; questioning
If she, too, were not under magic
Influence ; fearing almost a movement
The whole bright picture would dissipate.

    From an inner room close at hand, the
Kind old lady, we must henceforth know as
Mrs. Raymond, now drew near, in her
Hand a tiny waiter bearing, upon

Which were placed cookies and a glass of
Home-made wine, of which she pressed her guest
To partake, and which she did with thanks.
　" Forgive me if over-rude I seem :
But a woman's curiosity, you
Know, is proverbial ; and I am not
From others of my sex exempt.
As I entered, upon the door-plate
I saw inscribed a name which I conclude
Must be yours : therefore, if I mistake
Not, you are Mrs. Raymond ; and yonder
Is your daughter, the fair musician
To whose charming powers I am
Indebted for the treat I, a stranger,
Am enjoying ? "
　" I see," said Mrs. Raymond ; " you are in
Truth ' a Yankee,' most excellent at
Guessing ; though some features of the case
You've not rightfully hit. —
" Stella, darling, are you rested yet ?
If so, come sit beside me, while I
Somewhat of ourselves relate to this
Pleasant-looking lady, who, my heart
Tells me, will soon become to us a
Friend."
　Stella, approaching, bowed with graceful
Ease ; and on an ottoman at her
Grandma's knee she sat, her head reclining
In her lap. " Stella Graham," resumed
The old lady, " is the only
Daughter of my only daughter, and
From early childhood has been bereft
Of parental care ; though I have e'er

Striven to make for her the orphan's
Wants unknown." From those soft blue eyes the
Tear-drops fell amid the silken tresses
Of her pet, whom she caressed while talking.
" She is a slender child," she added :
" Still, when quite an infant, the strongest
Love for music she betrayed.
We are not wealthy, as you see : and
Yet we need not to complain ; since we
Have enough for all our needs. But she,
My Stella, for years one wish has cherished, —
To be a public singer ; and for
That purpose she has toiled until
Perfected in the art she's chosen.
And now, when fame seemed within her grasp,
Her health has failed ; and, by advice of
Our physician, we hither came last
Spring. Strangers in the place, but few there
Are whom we call *friend*. I had hoped much
From change of climate and the waters
So medicinal ; but, to my seeming,
She grows weaker day by day. As you see,
She is quite weary from just that little
Song to which you listened. O my darling,
My beautiful darling! what have I
Done that God should so scourge me ? "
    " Hush, dear grandma ! " said Stella, wiping
From her old friend's face the falling tears.
" You know I am quite reconciled at
Last to the dear Lord's will ; and what does
It matter, after all, the few more
Years of life ? Besides, you promised, dear
Grandmamma, to ever remember

My favorite Psalm : ' The Lord my shepherd
Is : I shall not want.   He maketh me
To lie down in green pastures ; he leadeth
Me beside the still waters ; he restoreth
My soul ; he leadeth me in the paths
Of righteousness for his name's sake.
Yea, though I walk through the valley of
The shadow of death, I will fear no
Evil : for thou art with me ; thy rod
And thy staff they comfort me.
Thou preparest a table before
Me in presence of mine enemies ;
Thou anointest my head with oil ;
My cup runneth over.   Surely
Goodness and mercy shall follow me
All the days of my life, and I will
Dwell in the house of the Lord forever.'
   " He has stilled my troubled soul with his
Promises so beautiful and full
Of hope," she added, turning to Sarah.
" My heart was very hard at first.   I
Could not, without many pangs, renounce
The inborn wish of my heart.   Music
Has been and is the one love of my life :
E'en paradise will be no haven
Of bliss, if Music's pæans sound not
Within the jasper gate.   Ah ! there *must* be
Music there, more grand and holy than
Mortal ears can e'er divine ! "
   Sarah's eyes upon the glowing face
Of the enraptured girl's were fastened ;
For never had they seen beauty so
Sublime.
   9*

" Fate once more has proved my friend," she said,
Arising to depart, " in leading
Me to you. You will not refuse me
Welcome if again I trespass ? " she
Questioned with anxious voice.
" Indeed, no ! " they both exclaimed : " come in
Whene'er you wish." With mutual kind
Wishes, they parted ; Sarah leaving
Upon a bracket a card-board
Lettered thus, — " Miss Sarah Horton,
Warwick, Massachusetts."

CHAPTER XX.

SARAH became with the passing days
A regular visitant at the cottage ;
To the inmates of which she became
Endeared. With their permission, Cornie
And Glencora both were frequent guests,
And, with Sarah, were quite enraptured
With the lovely Stella and her stately
Grandame. Their purest hours of pleasure
Were passed within that cosey home, so
Pregnant with the peace of holy lives.
The invalid was oft their companion
In pleasant walks and drives about the
Town, though oft the hectic flush burned upon
Her cheek. By mutual assent, they
Dear Mrs. Raymond styled " Mamma,"
And to her appealed in all their little
Trials, as daughters ever do to
A mother well beloved.
One morn, the rest of her party
Having joined an excursion to Glen's
Falls, Sarah entered the pretty home
Of her friends, and found them for a walk
Prepared, and, on inquiry, learned they
To church were going ; so her they asked
To join with them in the coming service.

For the first time, our friend listened to
The beautiful and soul-inspiring
Church ritual. Tears filled her eyes, while
Her very soul seemed like ocean-billows
Heaving. What was this strange religion,
So new to her experience, yet so
Grandly solemn? She crossed the threshold
Of Bethesda Church, heedless, truth to
Say, uncaring for its sacred rites:
She left it with an arrow in her
Soul, barbed at every point. Thought
Was awakened; and yet no word she
Breathed to those around, their comments dreading.

   October, with her gorgeous drapery,
Mantled the Eastern States, warning the
Pleasure-seekers that Summer's reign was
Over. The large hotels were closed; and
Our bridal-party prepared to bid
Adieu to Saratoga and her pleasant
Nooks. On the fourth day of the month,
Upon the morn of their departure,
Gordon and his fiancée were most
Quietly united in wedlock's
Holy bonds. The rector of the church
Episcopal the ceremony performed,
With no witnesses save their own party,
Including Stella and her grandma.
By this arrangement, Sarah was left
Decidedly *de trop ;* and, having really
No home-ties to draw her hence, she, by
Invitation kind of her new-found friends,
Decided to remain a while with
Them. By urgent request of Charles Stevens,

The tourists, the intervening weeks
Ere Christmas, would pass at the dear old
Home in N., where great preparations
Even then were being made for their
Reception.
    Now Sarah's life flowed in a different
Channel from its olden groove.
Such quiet hours of perfect peace had
Ne'er before fallen to her lot.
    She to Stella taught the art of
Imitating God's handiwork of
Flowers ; though poor indeed the little
Worsted imitations looked beside
His glowing blooms : but time it served to
While, and brightened many an hour.
In return, Stella feasted Sarah's
Soul with music. The old masters seemed
To breathe again 'neath her touch : those hands
So white and slender were endowed with
A glorious gift, such strains commanding
As sent sweet thrillings hot and fast through
Sarah's frame.
    From the re-action of such a moment
One night, Sarah clasped her friend
Closely to her throbbing, aching heart,
And exclaimed, " You *must* not, *shall* not, die !
I will so importune our Lord, he
Will death's fiat arrest, and you restore
Once again to health ; or, if some
Sacrifice is needed, I'll him beseech
Myself to take in place of you :
Any thing, rather than your dear form,
So beautiful and fair, shall fade and

Mould beneath the coffin-lid.   O God!
Hear thou my anguished prayer, and let
Me die for her!   But few would miss me
Long ; and no work here that I could do
Would be so great as my life giving
Up for hers.   Think of her rich gifts by
Thee bestowed ; of her young heart with
Devotion filled ; of all her pure, grand
Thoughts crushed out in silence of the
Grave ! ''
   " Cease, dear friend! " Stella answered back.
" Against our Lord you do blaspheme when
Thus you speak ; for we are his, to do
With as he wills.   My darling, I see
Your heart is very selfish ; and the
Creature 'tis you love, and not the Creator.
Bitter sorrows as your lips have quaffed,
They yet must drain more bitter still.
'Tis the fiery furnace alone that
Cleanses.   Now listen.   On that day when
First we met, you said 'twas Fate that brought
You here ; and, if 'twas Fate, then God is
Fate, and we are walking as he wills.
Some purpose of his own, to us unrevealed,
Has formed this friendship more than dear, and
On your part a worship wild.   Be governed
By his hand ; your heart submit to his
Decree : and be assured that whate'er
Is, is so to be ; and we can nothing
Change.   This poor body, lovely as you
Deem it, is not yours or mine, but his ; the
Gifts that he has with me crowned, whene'er
He wills, must honor his commands.

CHANGES. 107

'Up there' he has for me some work to
Do, — greater far than my mission here
Could be. Perhaps 'tis through your very
Love for me, your heart, so long rebellious,
Is touched into submission : loving
Me, you my home will love, and thus your
Thoughts become familiar with the life beyond."
   "Oh, consolation ! — you are indeed
My consolation ! " the weeping Sarah cried.
   The days and weeks rolled on. "Mamma" and
Her friend, with wistful eyes, saw the light
Slowly fading from their darling's face ;
And mutely questioned each of each, "How
Long, how long ? " She did not suffer much ;
And for that they were thankful: but like
A lovely flower, yielding, as it
Faded, its sweetest perfume ; so did
Stella fill their hearts with the holy
Richness of her dying hours. Tears seemed
Out of place in that room of peace.

   The short November day to its close
Was drawing, when Stella, rousing from
Her half-conscious state, wished to gaze once
More from the western window. The clouds
Seemed all aflame with tints of orange
And vermilion cast by the setting
Sun : and, as her dying eyes rested
Upon the heaven's panorama, a
Look of glory shone o'er all her face,
And with clasped hands she slowly said,
" *And there shall be no more night.*"

As the sun's slant rays on the far-off
Tree-tops lingered, she closed her eyes,
Murmuring low, " When next he comes, I
Shall be away.   Sarah, hold me in
Your arms once more; and, while the
Twilight shadows creep o'er all the earth,
Let me thank you for your tender care
Of me through these long, weary hours: and
If 'tis possible for spirits of
Those gone before to earthward come, then
Will I some day return to you, and
On your brow my hand will press " (thus
Laying her waxen hand on Sarah's
Face) ; " and you will know 'tis me, because
I'll whisper in your ear, ' Consolation ! '
    " Grandmamma, dear grandmamma ! " the dying
Angel said, " weep not for Stella much ;
And you will not be alone, since our
God-given friend will still be yours.   Death
Is nothing.   Imagine a river
Two states dividing, called mortal and immortal.
Upon this river a boat is moored ;
And those who would or *must* cross over
The helmsman hail, called Death ; and he will
Row us across the heaving tide, safe
Landing us upon the shore immortal.
And there, there, is rest.   Yes, there, too, is
Music, heaven-born.   I can hear the
Strains even now ; cannot you ? " turning
Her death-filmed eyes upon Sarah's face.
" Strange you cannot hear it too !   It is sweet, —
Sweeter far than aught of earth.   Truly,

' To Father, Son, and Holy Ghost,
 The God whom we adore,
Be glory as it was, is now,
 And shall be evermore.' "

The beautiful lips were closed, never
Again to open in this life ; the
Eyes, eloquent till death, were now sealed
Forever, their long lashes resting
Upon a cheek like marble ; about
The mouth a soft smile lingered, and the
Waxen hands still clasped as though in prayer.
 " She has reached the shore immortal,"
Sarah whispered to the kneeling woman
By her side. " Our darling has passed on ;
And *we* are left. See ! how happy is
Her smile ! how beautiful, *how* beautiful,
She looks ! — my sweet, my blessed consolation ! "

 After Stella within the tomb was
Placed, Mamma Raymond went to C., the
Coming winter to pass with relatives.
The pretty cottage was closed ; and to
The door a placard was attached,
" For sale."
 Sarah to her olden life returned
Again ; the same, yet not the same.
Changes had wrought their influence on
Her heart, in which one idol was
Enshrined, one memory of a pure
Friendship, surpassing that of Hymen's
Vow, — the dream of her woman's heart, when
Every nerve within her being vibrated

10

To the touch of those slender hands so
Loving in their clasp, and on whose brow
The sorrowing girl a crown of love
Had placed; and 'mid the leaves embalmed
Were twined the words, " My consolation."

CHAPTER XXI.

CONCLUSION.

VISIT with us once again the pleasant
Farm-house of Uncle Nathan, whose laugh
Resounds as gayly through the house as
When, a youth, he brought his bright-eyed wife
To dwell with him years agone.   And can
It be, the social, gentlemanly
Master of the house is the once-
Bashful Charles?   Where now has fled his
Olden disdain for the ladies ?
Echo answers, " Where ? "   And Cornie, fair
As summer morn, is of her husband's heart
The queen, as of all the household.   A
Precious hope now thrills her heart with joy
For the future ; while Charles's step more
Manly grows while dreaming of the *May
Be*.   Gordon and his beloved Glencora
Are in their olden home at W.
He with lavish hand the manna
Of life imparting to those who will
Partake ; enjoying in the sweets of home
The happiness that ever crowns hopes
Long deferred, when at last they realize
Their fruition.
  Visiting in N., Sarah was one evening
Startled by her cousin's saying, " There

Is to be, this week, a lecture upon
' The Times,' from a young man of more than
Ordinary ability : you remember
Him, cousin, — our old friend, Harry
Golding ? " — " Yes, she remembered, and would
The lecture most certainly attend ; "
Which proved to be rich with cultured thought.
A thrill of honest pride through her ran
As she listened to the warm words of
Eloquence which from the lips of this
Dark-browed speaker fell ; thinking, " He once
Loved me, plain and humble ; and I have
Been the means of stirring into life
The electric wells of thought with which
This man was endowed, but which slumbered
Beneath the bond of pleasure.   One good
Deed I can to myself accredit."
    As on former days, he was invited
By her cousin home ; which invitation,
With a glance at Sarah, he accepted.
During their walk from the hall, questions
Were exchanged, and answers given.   Just
As they entered the house, his hand was
Laid on Sarah's arm with gentle force,
While with voice suppressed, yet eager, he
Said, " Here, where the motto was to me
Given, I the same restore with its
Added crown ; fondly hoping
The mistress of my heart that word will
Supplant with the dearer one of love.
Which shall it be, dear friend ? "
    " Harry, excelsior is from me
A kinder word than love, and you the
Same must keep.   I have for you none other."

October, soft and solemn in her
Wearing, again the earth was carpeting
With a garment rare, when Sarah's foot
Pressed the streets of Saratoga on a
Pilgrimage of love.   Up to the
Cemetery her steps she wended
To the spot where she and " Mamma " had
Caused to be erected a plain white
Slab over the dear remains of one
To them beloved.   Anon her hand upon
The stone was pressed, on which was graven
An open book, and on its marble
Page was cut a rose with scattered leaves.
Above the book a slender hand was
Poised, with index-finger raised.   By the
Hand a ribbon-scroll was held, bearing
On one end the name and age ; upon
The other, the word, " Consolation."
    Next to that grave, Bethesda Church was
To her heart the dearest spot she knew.
Many have been her silent vigils
At either shrine.   Long her stubborn heart
Refused to be comforted, yet e'er
Beseeching help ; when, like a vision
Of the morn at day-dawn, her soul caught
The radiance of our Father's love,
And was bathed in the light thereof.
Daily she wandered by the
To her sacred grave, living o'er once
Again that friendship, sudden in its
Bloom, ardent and changeless to the end.
Behold her now as the slant rays of

The setting sun shine athwart the grave,
With hands clasped, and eyes upraised to the
Heaven's blue ether, whither her darling
Has gone ! *She waits for the unseen hand*
Her brow to press, and for her soul's
Assurance of " CONSOLATION."